The
Magic
of
Mind Power

"Every man who knows how to read has it in his power to magnify himself, to multiply the ways in which he exists, to make his life full, significant and interesting." Aldous Huxley

"Mind is the living quality of life itself. It is eternal." Barrie Konicov

The
Magic
of
Mind Power

Awareness Techniques
for the
Creative Mind

by

Duncan McColl

Crown House Publishing Limited

Published in the UK by

Crown House Publishing
Crown Buildings
Bancyfelin
Carmarthen
Wales

First published 1985
by GATEWAY BOOKS, Bath.

British Library of Cataloguing-in-Publication Data
A catalogue entry for this book is available
from the British Library.

ISBN 1899836292

Printed and bound in Wales by
WBC Book Manufacturers,
Waterton Industrial Estate,
Bridgend, Mid Glamorgan.

Contents

The book is dedicated:

- to my patient guides and teachers, many of whom are quoted in the following pages.

- to the most patient of them all, Mary, my wife, who alone gives life a purpose.

- to Peter, my son, who learned early to take the rough with the rough and to Rilla, who also made DCMcC Jnr. and Jennifer possible.

- to all fellow pilgrims, pathfinders, bondbreakers and to The Great Illusionist, for the current trip, this merry mosaic of fumbles, follies, frolics and fun.

What is a woman's basic need in life?
Y̶o̶u̶ ̶w̶i̶l̶l̶ ̶f̶i̶n̶d̶ ̶t̶h̶e̶ ̶a̶n̶s̶w̶e̶ You will not
find the answer in this book . . .

Introduction

Only you can reawaken the magical powers of your own creative mind, and the easiest and most effective way of doing so is by consciously developing the natural self-hypnotic skills that you unconsciously use every day of your life.

To this extent, all men are created equal: each of us has access to unlimited positive potential. There are no exceptions. The creative channels of mind can be cleared to enable us to harmonise and focus the two greatest mental forces available to mankind: imagination and desire. When imagination is subconsciously in conflict with desire, imagination always wins. When both these forces are co-ordinated, anything worthwhile is possible.

By using simple self-hypnotic techniques to enable you to relax creatively in any circumstances, you reawaken a profound dynamism of the self. Positive improvements in your health, energy, attitudes and creative abilities are immediately evident.

No dependence on anyone else is required and there are no dangers whatsoever in developing the skill. There is not, and there never has been, any possibility with self-hypnosis of being controlled or manipulated against your will or induced unwittingly into a deep state of trance. In fact, for hypnosis to be effective, you must decide to relax and you must consciously choose and earnestly desire to make a specific change in your behavioural patterns.

Thanks to negative mental programming in the past and to stressful living conditions, the conscious and subconscious levels of mind are too often out of phase or even working

1

strenuously against one another. Your head and your heart are at war. The seemingly magical healing and other results of self-hypnosis are simply achieved by relaxing and allowing the conscious and control levels of mind to move into harmony and balance, unifying, concentrating and focusing your full mental powers to achieve a heightened state of general awareness and control. When this elevated state of mind is effortlessly achieved with self-hypnosis, your conscious yearnings and desires cease to be frustrated by your own subconscious fears, doubts and superstitions.

In other respects, the obvious fact is that we were not all created equal. The truth is that we were all created unique. And the exceptionally successful and talented people of the world differ from the rest in only one respect. Their uniqueness, their individuality, was encouraged and developed, not inhibited and suppressed. Self-hypnosis techniques enable you to reawaken your own uniquely creative talents. They provide the key to your powerhouse mind. This is your birthright. It is never too late to claim it.

Once started the process unfolds quite naturally. Your visualisation skills increase with practice. You find that you can relax and visualise as clearly as you do in your dreams. Your creative imagination and your intuitive powers develop to whatever level you desire. Once the way is known, the self-imposed limitations of the old, low-level viewpoint simply drop away and life is seen from a refreshingly new vantage point.

'Can we see ourselves as others see us? Can I personally control my life and my destiny? Can I eliminate all self-destructive habits right now? Can I ensure my health, wealth and happiness and success in all things? And more?' The answer, as you will soon find out, is a most emphatic 'yes'. Resolve to postpone any habitual feelings of disbelief and decide to find out for yourself. Beliefs and disbeliefs are of no significance whatsoever unless you can put them to practical use in improving the way you live.

Thanks to the introduction of audio cassettes, the acceptance of the beneficial influences of self-hypnosis techniques are breaking through those two common barriers to human evolution, ignorance and fear. Progress has also been retarded over the centuries by many who were well aware of the unlimited potential for self-development through hypnosis, but who were equally well aware that their own influence and incomes would be diminished by its general introduction and use. Their personal concern was well justified because self-hypnosis introduces a new form of dependence. You learn to depend on yourself.

Good health is not something you can buy or rely on someone else to provide.

From TM to Zen, from shamanism to the Nembutsu rituals of Buddhism, the essential ingredient is always some form of self-hypnosis developed from the teachings of Hermes Trismegistus about 800 BC. Hermes, the Master of Masters, originated the visualisation techniques to attain what he identified as the fourth state of consciousness. Most successful mantra and prayer techniques were doubtless derived from the same source but as religions became commercialised, prayers became a part of the bell, book and candle routines and lost their original purpose, the attainment of deeper personal awareness and expanded consciousness.

Other variations on self-hypnosis today include biofeedback and alphawave induction techniques to demonstrate the immediate influences that thought can have on the body.

Apart from dozens of covert variations which depend more for their effect on drugs, hypnosis turns out to be the main spring for many reputable self-development practices including ESP, Silva Mind Control and other 'scientific self-suggestion' and relaxation therapy programmes.

If your medical adviser has done his homework on self-hypnosis techniques he will happily confirm that healing is greatly accelerated by inducing a 'wakeful hypermetabolic physiological state of mind'.

Hypnosis, Fact and Fancy

"I read the newspapers avidly. They are my one form of continuous fiction." (Aneurin Bevan)

Though hypnosis is a natural skill which is inherent in everyone, some people are naturally more accomplished than others and need little guidance or instruction. The more intelligent and imaginative a person the easier it is to master the skill. A weak-willed person, accustomed to the domination of others, must first be awakened to seek truth and strength in himself.

Hypnosis is basically a technique for focusing awareness and at the same time broadening perception to appreciate the full spectrum of events and see beyond the merely superficial. Practice results in focusing and fine-tuning the mind so that all mental, bodily and spiritual levels function in harmony.

Most of the beneficial effects of hypnosis are attainable at a light level of relaxation or trance equivalent to the mental state experienced in day-dreaming or in becoming absorbed in an interesting novel or film.

All hypnosis is essentially self-hypnosis. A hypnotist or hypnotic recording can guide you to introduce the hypnotic state. If you decide to be receptive to the suggestions — and only then — a state of relaxation can be induced to facilitate the shift of your awareness from outer to inner consciousness, from cortical to sub-cortical levels of mind. You can choose at any time to override the relaxation suggestions and you will not respond to hypnosis.

Subliminal recordings are today available in which carefully selected beneficial phrases and affirmations are directed to the sub-cortical levels, by-passing the critical or analytical screen of the conscious mind. The technique does not involve hypnosis. Later, a simple routine will be explained which eliminates the possibility of being influenced by any form of subliminal suggestions to which you may be unwittingly exposed. A natural safeguard exists to the extent that frequent repetition of subliminal messages is necessary to achieve lasting effects. The advantage in using subliminal recordings, particularly in language training and similar applications, is that, unlike self-hypnosis tapes, they can be used while driving or engaged in any routine activity.

Hypnotic States of Mind

A common fallacy is that people lose all control under hypnosis and can be made to react as the hypnotist dictates. Even at the deeper levels of hypnosis required, for example, in the suppression of severe pain, as one part of the mind becomes relaxed and inattentive, another part becomes increasingly aware. In fact, awareness reaches a level many times greater than that experienced in the state we call 'normal awakening consciousness'. This leads many people to the mistaken belief that they are not actually hypnotised and self-induced tests are necessary to convince them that the required level of relaxation has been reached. Hypnosis expands the levels of ordinary consciousness, widening perception and deepening your power of introspection, it does not cause you to lose consciousness.

If the circumstances are appropriate, you may choose to drift into a light hypnotic sleep. This is entirely acceptable because your subconscious mind never sleeps and you will continue to absorb the recorded or spoken messages, awakening fully refreshed at whatever time you have chosen.

A simple hypnotic technique is used to enable you to return to normal awakening consciousness at any predetermined time. However, in the event of any form of emergency, the enhanced awareness ensures that you will respond instantly in a calm, effective and confident manner. Your subconscious mind is deeply concerned with your survival and invariably acts to ensure it, as you will have experienced in driving when your conscious mind may have drifted to the extent that you fail to recall having passed a familiar landmark.

Practical Benefits of Self-Hypnosis

As at least eighty-per-cent of all physical and psychological health problems are stress-related, the greatest immediate benefit is that you will learn how to reduce tension and stress in your body and mind to tolerable levels. This, in turn, enables the subconscious to direct more positive energy to the performance of the autonomic functions, which control the general functioning and well-being of the entire body system. Excellent results are also obtained in treating a wide range of other mental and emotional problems, from habit control and phobia elimination to improving concentration, creativity and learning ability.

Stage Hypnotists: do they have special powers?

A stage hypnotist uses a simple screening technique to select the most hypnotically susceptible people in an audience, as his aim is to work quickly and superficially. He is a showman and his object is merely to amuse and entertain. No special powers or abilities are required.

The hypnotist or hynotherapist uses his knowledge and experience for therapeutic and educational purposes to stimulate your own inborn powers for achieving vibrant good health and success. The techniques can be conveyed in writing, verbally or by demonstration. In speaking, a normal conversational tone of voice is used: there is no call for the distractive gimmickry of the old-time stage hypnotist, any more than modern medical practitioners are expected to peddle bottles of home-brewed herbal tonic in the market-place.

Alpha-Wave Induction, Meditation, Prayer and Hypnosis

Each of these disciplines involves relaxation and either an expansion or focusing of awareness. Experience in any one can greatly facilitate understanding and accelerate success in any of the others. Hypnosis is the fastest and, through the medium of tape recordings, the most private, convenient and personally effective method of reaching an understanding, not only of how you function and why, but also of how little you require to do to improve your present health and general status in life. Hypnosis is not a belief system ... beneficial results are usually immediately apparent. Nor does it create the kind of dependency on others which can expose you to all kinds of cunning or unconscious manipulation.

An experienced hypnotist can guide you to eliminate or control a self-destructive habit within half-an-hour. No further instruction is normally needed. Similarly, playing a suitable self-hypnotic recording while you sleep can achieve the same satisfactory results. In either case, you will gain an understanding of the techniques of self-hypnosis which you can then use beneficially in hundreds of ways.

The power of the imagination, properly focused, is truly remarkable. What is equally remarkable is that so many people can drift aimlessly through life oblivious to that fact that they have ready access to unlimited personal power and potential.

Can everyone be hypnotised?

If you can be taught anything you can be taught how to use hypnotic techniques beneficially ... if you have the desire to learn. The old 'horse to water' rule applies here. For this reason, when you experience the first flush of success with hypnotism, be prepared to see that others fail to share your enthusiasm: never forget how long it took you to become interested, and why. The fact you are deeply aware that an unhealthy person would benefit immeasurably is never adequate motivation for them. Your feeling of compassion will not be wasted: be patient, the influence of your newly-awakened consciousness will become apparent. One picture of good health is worth more than ten thousand words.

Are there dangers in hypnosis?

There is a real danger to the hypnotist, as there is to all people involved in health care. The hypnotist can be adversely affected by the negative emanations from the subject: he can unwittingly absorb the negative vibrations. There is a simple and fully effective procedure for avoiding this very real negative influence which will be explained in detail later. Make no mistake: all forms of energy can be either friendly or unfriendly, depending upon how we use or abuse them. Through lack of understanding of our personal powers, we can hurt ourselves and others without knowing how or when we do it.

Hypnosis is a natural state of consciousness by which we have all been influenced at one time or another and often negatively. An experienced hypnotist and professional hypnotic tapes convey only positive messages which can only produce beneficial results. In brief, there is no danger or possibility of harmful results.

Mentally handicapped people or those experiencing chronic mental strain are best advised to use hypnotic techniques only after consultation with their medical advisers. Specific hypnotic techniques are required to prepare the subject to awaken slowly to the cause of the problem, which is invariably subconscious overreaction to a series of emotional shocks leading to a fleeing from life. Only an experienced hypnotist can guide the subject to identify and eliminate the subconscious cause.

The cassette tapes which will be described later in some detail all introduce a recommendation that they should not be played by anyone in a highly emotional state or undergoing treatment requiring medication, without first consulting a doctor. This is commendable because frankly it is inconceivable that tapes dealing with relaxation, insomnia, pain relief, weight reduction and a host of kindred subjects, because of the expertly chosen affirmations and positive nature, could have anything but positive beneficial results, despite the physical, mental or spiritual instability of the listener.

Needless to say, in driving a car or in other similar circumstances, the hypnotic state must not be induced. All self-hypnotic material includes this warning. Subliminal recordings can be played with advantage when driving or engaged in some routine activity such as housework. Not only is the subliminal message conveyed clearly to the subconscious control centre, the conscious mind is stimulated to increased alertness. You can prove this to yourself if you are tired and have a need to stay awake. Otherwise, avoid playing a subliminal recording at bedtime: you will find it very difficult to sleep.

Hypnosis and Healing

"The art of medicine consists of amusing the patient while Nature cures the disease". (Voltaire)

Hypnosis, as your experience will soon confirm, is always self-hypnosis, just as healing is always self-healing. A broken limb can be reset, for example, but it heals by itself. You recover from a serious illness only because you consciously and subconsciously want to recover. If you allow a hypnotist to use his skills in inducing a state of relaxation and serenity, you will become calm and mentally responsive to what he is saying. The three essential elements are motivation, relaxation and acceptance — nothing more is required.

If you have the desire and motivation to develop skill in self-hypnosis, you can use a simple relaxation technique and then make whatever positive affirmations or suggestions you wish to central control: to your subconscious mind. Dependence on a third-party is avoided. The problem with dependence is that, by relying on self-styled experts, we allow our own innate skills and capabilities to languish and decay to the extent that we easily fall victims to deception and exploitation.

Relaxation is essential to healthy and successful living, and this is a state of mind far removed from the customary state of incessant activity to which most minds are prone. Using self-hypnotic techniques, we can establish a neutral field and experience serenity at will without resort to alcohol, drugs and other chemicals which eventually destroy the body's natural resistance to pain and infection.

By conveying post-hypnotic suggestions to the subconscious mind while the chattering conscious level is relaxed, we encourage the natural curative forces to deal with any problem or malady in a direct, positive manner, freed from the confusion caused at superficial levels by negative influences, either imagined or real. For the time being, put aside any thoughts about 'mind over matter' and similar shallow concepts. It is nearer the truth to think in terms of providing an atmosphere in which the mind-body-spirit

10

"Now chaps .. all those in favour of Preventative Medicine!"

entity can become harmonised with the environment, rather than continue in its customary state of external conflict and internal civil war.

In group therapy, this positive atmosphere can be shared by all participants with mutually beneficial results or it can be channelled towards an individual with an immediate need for specific help. This channelling phenomenon by means of the group subsconscious produces results which are often reported as miracles or faith-healing. Unfortunately, many who have discovered how to focus these energies over the centuries have been regarded by powerful men as posing a threat to their manipulation and exploitation of the masses and the teachings have been ridiculed, distorted or physically suppressed.

The truth is that whether we use self-hypnosis techniques for our own benefit or channel the positive influences personally or in groups to others, each of us can achieve a high degree of proficiency in psychic healing. By understanding the simple functioning of the various levels of mind we can at least ensure that we never contribute negatively to anybody's physical or mental condition.

Have you ever been hypnotised?

Day-dreaming is a simple form of self-hypnosis in which we all indulge from time to time. The rhythm of a car engine and the humming sound that speeding tyres produce can together induce varying degrees of hypnosis, particularly when accompanied by monotonous motorway scenery. Absorption in a novel or a television presentation can also induce a hypnotic trance. As these occasions illustrate, you can become fully hypnotised though your eyes remain open, and this holds true even at the deeper levels.

If we all knew the extent to which self-hypnosis enters into the phenomenon of falling in love, much agony and many unhappy marriages could be avoided. 'Falling' is often a more aptly descriptive verb than we are aware of at the time.

As you read the next few dozen sentences, make yourself more comfortable, tense your neck, arms, shoulders — tense them now — and then relax them as fully as you can. Take a deep breath, then slowly exhale and imagine you are reading these words to someone sitting nearby. You are reading perhaps a little more slowly and clearly than you customarily speak. Clarity is assured if you place some stress or emphasis on the 'ess' sounds. Speak aloud if it is convenient to do so. And you are saying *"please relax now, as much as you can, and now listen closely and discover that just by listening you can relax even more. Tense and then relax each part of the body a little at a time, starting with the toes, tense them a little then just let them go limp, lazy, relaxed. And next, the rest of the foot, and the ankles, so that your ankles and feet feel limp, lazy and relaxed. And this sensation of relaxation rises up and passes to the legs, the knees, the thighs, progressing upwards slowly to the shoulders and back muscles, to the neck and head. Now as you are listening to my voice and only to my voice you will notice a stiffness in your jaw muscles and you will tense and relax your jaw – do it now. Sensing a dryness in your throat you will pause a moment to swallow and you will swallow now and go deeper into relaxation. Counting now from one to five, at the count of five you will become fully alert, feeling rested and revitalised ... one, two, three, four, five, fully awake, feeling great..!"*

If you are as susceptible to verbal persuasion as most of us are, you may have noticed that your own voice has a natural hypnotic effect, and you will have guessed the reason. All skillful manipulators introduce sibilant sounds in their speech to lull the mind into a state of ready suggestibility, of hypnosis. Watch how often this is used in advertising presentations. Incidentally, a competent hypnotist has no need to resort to trick vocabulary though he will tend, quite naturally, to avoid harsh sounding words and phrases, as inducing a state of relaxation is the aim. The need to use precise, literal phrases in guiding the subconscious is essential, as you will fully appreciate later.

How to relax and increase awareness

We can start with a simple relaxation technique that you can use any time you feel that relaxation and increased concentration are appropriate. It will enable you to conserve energy and focus the mind better when reading, studying or doing any monotonous or boring job. Do not allow your analytical mind to be misled by its simplicity. With practice, it will become a powerful weapon in your defence against distraction and similar negative or self-defeating attitudes and emotions.

The technique has a long and honourable history, dating back thousands of years before its adoption as an early Christian-Judaic prayer and meditation technique.

While reading the next several lines, place the book on a table or on your lap or hold it comfortably in your left hand. Allow your right arm to dangle limply by your side. Do that now, before reading on. Now check for tension by tensing your arms and shoulders and relax them. Inhale slowly and deeply, hold the breath to the mental count of four and release it in a long, deep sigh. Do it again if you choose to do so, counting down from eight to one as you slowly release the breath. Do this now. What follows can wait.

While continuing to read, become aware of the weight and the tingling sensation in the fingers of your right hand, be conscious of the heaviness as the blood flow gently pulses at the tips of the fingers, circulating freely without any conscious effort on your part. Just be aware of your fingers, do not concentrate on them. Just be conscious of the heaviness and the pleasant tingling sensation. You are reading these words and at deeper level you are becoming conscious of the tingling sensation and your concentration on the words is automatically becoming deeper. After you have read the next three sentences you will allow your eyes to close normally and naturally while you are still aware of the tingling sensation in your fingers. After you close your eyes you will count slowly from one to five, and at the count of five the tingling sensation will cease, your eyes will open and you will return to normal awakening consciousness, feeling pleasantly refreshed and relaxed. Now allow your eyes to close and count up from one to five.

Good. You will appreciate that the benefits of this ancient technique follow from practising it whenever you have a free moment. There is no need to close your eyes, merely breathe deeply and sense your fingers, be aware of them while sitting, resting or walking. Check for yourself the influence the procedure has on your mental alertness, for example when you are attending a dull business meeting or performing some routine task. In fact, at any time at work or play when you feel your interest and attention flagging for any reason.

Check the effect whenever you feel influenced by any strong negative emotion such as depression, loneliness, fear, anger, sorrow, or boredom. Particularly be alert to influences which occur some time after using this or any other positive hypnotic technique. They may be subtle enough to pass virtually unnoticed, but they can provide feedback on the effectiveness of this simple awareness technique. There is nothing wrong in finding an occasional smile on your face instead of the frown and tenseness of jaw which could unconsciously be accepted as your customary pose. Check the tension in your jaw now, waggle it a bit and relax. Was it tensed?

Ten minutes of relaxing with this sensing technique can replace as much lost energy as several hours of stressful sleep. The method also has the virtue of pointing up several of the aspects of self-hypnotism which, consciously or unconsciously, can cause concern to the timid or superstitious. You do not lose control of yourself, you become *more* rather than less alert at both the conscious and subconscious levels of mind. You can enter and leave the harmonious state of mind whenever you choose to do so. Nobody can hypnotise you against your will, but you can consciously hypnotise yourself. What practice in self-hypnosis will soon reveal to you is that you are continuously exposed to negative hypnotism. Becoming aware of this fact and of the simple techniques for avoiding it provides the key that unlocks the door that you allowed to be closed on your own unlimited positive potential.

Self-hypnosis induction procedure 'A'

"Body and soul are not two substances but one. They are man becoming aware of himself in two different ways!" (C.F. Von Weizsacker)

To achieve a satisfactory level of relaxation will normally take less than half the time it will take you to read the following guidelines.

Initially, select a time and place where you can be reasonably free from distractions and make yourself comfortable.

Loosen any tight clothing and resolve that for the next few minutes you are going to devote yourself to achieving a gentle state of relaxation, of letting go.

With practice, you will find that you can use this and later techniques for relaxing in whatever situations of stress or strain you may encounter.

Absorb the general theme of the following four paragraphs so that you can go through the exercise without having to read it:

1. Centre. This means relax by inhaling as deeply as you

comfortably can, hold the breath for the mental count of four, then exhale slowly in a long, deep sigh, allowing your eyes to close normally and naturally. Repeat this if necessary before reverting to your customary breathing rhythm.

2. At the count of three, visualise the sunlight shining down on your body, focusing it as you would the beam of a flashlight, relaxing the muscles as you direct the light up and down the right arm. Now move the beam of light to the left arm, then to each leg in turn. Next direct the light to the stomach and feel it glow as it enters and moves to the chest, to the head and then right down the full length of the spine and

3. feel the light radiate ... radiate ... radiate ... through every bone in your body, and feel every nerve, muscle, cell and sinew bathed in the warm glow of the light ... and relax. Relax.

4. Count from one to five and, at the count of 'five', return to full awakening consciousness.

With experience, what seems to require a special effort in visualisation will become easier each time, as the mind learns to respond consciously to instructions to perform a function which it habitually performs unconsciously. Any initial difficulties will be remembered with amusement as you move effortlessly to higher levels of awareness and mental control.

You will become more conscious of the ceaseless chattering of the mind as you seek to relax completely, but make no effort to suppress it. Be aware of it in the same way that you would respond to the excited chirpings of starlings as they settle for the night. The mental static will eventually diminish and fade into the background.

Ignore any mental promptings that the exercise is too simple to be of practical value. The rational or conscious mind is the father and mother of all our illusions, and it will play whatever tricks it can devise to avoid being recognised for the cunning trickster it is. It has become conditioned to deceive us in hundreds of subtle ways, each designed to separate us from our originality.

Hypnotic deepening techniques

Inhaling deeply and retaining the breath may initially prove difficult for some. Do the best you comfortably can. Self-torture games of any kind are to be avoided.

For those who experience no discomfort, inhale and release the breath slowly, once or twice, to the mental count of eight to one, thus: *"eight .. seven .. going down, deeper .. six .. five .. deeper .. four, three, two, one ... zero, zero, zero."* As you count down with the eyes closed, becoming more and more relaxed, press the tips of the index finger and thumb of each hand gently together as you mentally repeat *"zero"*, adding *"Relax ... serenity"* or whatever keywords you prefer.

As you inhale you may occasionally find it helpful to tense the fists and relax them as you slowly exhale.

Visualising

Your reaction to being asked to bring the sunlight down around your body will give you an insight as to how receptive you are to suggestion, and how far out of touch or in harmony you are with your powers of imagination. Whatever the initial reaction, these powers can be fine-tuned to a higher degree. The more proficient you become in using your visualisation skills, the closer you come to the source of your unlimited potential.

Occasionally, as you exhale and count down from eight to zero, visualise the numbers. Alternatively, visualise a second countdown while breathing normally. Allow the descending numbers to float into your awareness, taking whatever time is necessary. Never be concerned if some or all of the numbers are reluctant to surface. They will eventually appear as effortlessly as the images you experience in your dreams.

Later on, the speed and clarity with which the numbers appear will give a good indication of how much in harmony you are with the deeper creative levels of mind. You may also become more aware of the extent to which alcohol and other temporary stimulants dull or distort access to the creative mind.

Visualisation skills can be renewed by scores of other exercises, offsetting the effect of television in turning us into visual illiterates. Staying with the numbers theme, you can visualise them increasing or decreasing in size or appearing in various colours. Another procedure is to cut out of paper a blue square, a green triangle and a red circle and fix them at eye level to a wall or the inside of a cupboard door that you can open when you practise. Follow the breathing and relaxation routine, then focus the eyes on, say, the red circle. Then close the eyes and visualise the colour and the design as though you were looking from a point in the centre of your forehead. Do the same with the square and the triangle. Then interchange the colours and designs in your imagination. For self-healing and personal success, there is no need to attain this level of proficiency in visualisation, but if you find that you have retained these capabilities since childhood, they will prove invaluable for many purposes which will be explained later.

Conclude each practice session by centering, relaxing and affirming: *"Whenever I count from eight to zero I will relax ten times more deeply and I will visualise clearly whatever I wish to bring to mind."*

Focusing mind power, induction procedure 'B'

Spiritual masters of many traditions have referred to the intellectual programmed mind as the monkey mind. Professor Fritz Perls, father of gestalt therapy, preferred to refer to it as the garbage pail. Either way, their aim is to alert us to the fact that the conditioned mind, albeit essential to maintaining or improving our status on the social scene, is disastrous in the role of master. Decide — and you can — decide to set fifteen minutes aside from the hurly-burly world to dedicate to the following exercise. Fifteen minutes.

Select any small object with which you are familiar. A simple glass or metal object is most appropriate.

Briefly, the exercise involves six stages: study the object, centre, open the eyes while still centered to restudy the object, close the eyes and visualise, then exit from hypnosis. Do a dummy run through the procedure before centering and closing the eyes. Use the finger sensing technique to improve your concentration while reading. The six stages are as follows:

1. Examine the object as closely as you can for up to five minutes, as though you were seeing it for the first time. Notice details that you have not bothered to notice before. Five minutes.

2. Centre, breathe deeply, count down, relax and allow the eyes to close. Repeat the centering technique to ensure a satisfactory depth of relaxation, of letting go.

3. Affirm: *"I will count to three and reopen my eyes to study the object, remaining relaxed and alert. After two minutes study, my eyes will close and I will clearly visualise the object. Counting: one, two, three, eyes are open for two minutes."*

4. Eyes close......

5. Visualise.......

6. Exit, counting from one to five.

A variation is to visualise the object as at stage five and go there, enter the object in your imagination. How does it feel to be the object: comfortable, warm, lonely? Reach forward and fondle the object. Then exit from hypnosis.

Do you feel a different relationship with the object now that you know it better? Have you seen its hidden facets? If you have succeeded in relating closely to it while you were relaxed and open, your deeper feelings for it will always remain.

Devote some time to repeating the exercise at a later date, possibly choosing a vase of flowers or a plant as the object of study.

Merely reading about the exercise, and thinking that you can benefit without actually experiencing it, will only add strength to that part of the mind which is already over-stimulated and over-inflated, the conditioned intellect. This is the same superficial level of mind which comforts us with the thought that we can resolve our frustrations and problems by talking or thinking about them, instead of seeking to understand what causes them. By these simple exercises we gradually renew our contact with the higher levels of consciousness, which awaken to the need to play a more active role in distinguishing between real and imaginary influences at the surface levels of our reality.

During the exercise, you may have become aware of a variation in the frequency of distracting thoughts which arose when focusing the attention consciously, and later in the more relaxed mode. The procedure can be adapted and used effectively for resolving problems. This is possible because problems caused at the superficial levels of mind are never solved at the same shallow levels. By relaxing under mild hypnosis and reviewing the problem at the deeper levels, the solution automatically surfaces. No need arises to press for a solution: as the negative distractions of anxiety and frustration are removed, the mental vision clears and the solution becomes apparent.

From a divided and confused mind, only more confusion can arise. When you have developed a unified centre of control, a mental 'safe house' from which to function, you will find that sound decisions become easier to make.

The effect of these preliminary exercises is cumulative and repetition will result in a greater degree of objectivity and detachment from extraneous thoughts. Be alert to the cunning of the analytical and judgmental mind — the same conditioned level — in expecting too much too soon. Particularly ignore any promptings which flow from preconceived notions of the depth of the trance state.

Beneficial suggestions and affirmations best reach the subconscious control levels of mind at the light levels of trance which we all experience in the process of falling asleep. We pass through these same levels on awakening. By 'cat-napping', Winston Churchill, Albert Einstein, Henry Ford and other remarkable men learned how to tap the subconscious sources of physical and mental power. You may have hoped to resolve a personal problem by sleeping on it and have been disappointed with the result. Part of the reason, as mentioned earlier, is that the majority of us fail to relax fully even when we sleep. Our consciousness merely shifts to a lower level of tension than the one we have accustomed ourselves to accept as normal. Consequently, night and day, vital energy is dissipated or diverted from the renovation and renewal of the multitude of physical, mental and spiritual aspects of our being, all of which are required to contribute continuously to our general good health and sense of well-being.

The more we subject ourselves to tension throughout the day, the more disturbed our sleep, and the less capable we become in coping with the following day. The circle of events closes on itself and, as will be explained in some detail later, the normal compensations and remedies we seek at this stage only serve to suppress or disguise the symptoms. The accepted treatment is as sensible as replacing a fuse without checking to see where the electrical circuit is faulty. The source of the problem remains and the negative influence is left to grow in strength.

Hypnotic induction procedure 'C'

As you practice the induction procedures, be careful to avoid articulating or allowing your tongue to form the words. Messages are best conveyed to the subconscious as impressions or mental pictures. The feeling and spirit of the message is what counts, not the repetition of doggerel. As children, we are taught to associate sounds with what we see and experience, to enable us to communicate. Later we fall into the trap of allowing our emotions to be triggered by words, giving them a reality they can never possess.

To achieve a satisfactory level of relaxation, there is nothing new to do. As you become aware of the nature of the distractions to which you are presently exposed, they will cease of their own accord.

Our linear process of thought, and the further limitation imposed by written communication, both pose difficulties in conveying new concepts of sensory awareness. In performing this and some subsequent exercises, three options are open to you.

The first is to study the text until you become sufficiently conversant with the general theme to implement it without further recourse to the script. It may prove helpful to summarise the salient features in your own words. Using a relaxation technique, you will experience a steady improvement in your ability to concentrate, absorb and later recall what you have read.

The second alternative is to use a recorder to tape the message verbatim, later playing it back as you relax and follow the taped instructions. You should speak in the normal tone of voice you would use in general conversation.

Lacking recording facilities, you will find it mutually beneficial to swop the roles of reader and listener with someone who shares your interest.

The procedure is a progressive relaxation technique, designed to deepen the level of relaxation. It was devised by Barrie Konicov, one of the greatest living masters of hypnotherapy. His teachings permeate this work and there will be occasion to introduce him to you more fully later. This exercise is particularly appropriate for those who are well oriented in their feelings.

Find yourself in a comfortable position, seated in a chair, your feet firmly on the floor, your hands open and palms upwards on your lap. Begin by taking a long, slow, deep breath through the nose, allowing your eyes to close normally and naturally. Hold the breath for the mental count of four, open your mouth, and as you exhale all the air from your body, mentally count from eight to one and let go. Excellent.

Now place your awareness in your feet and experience your feet beginning to sink into the floor. Create a feeling of heaviness in your feet. Create it so completely that, in a few minutes time, it will require a great deal of effort even to try to lift your legs. Feel your legs growing heavier and heavier by the minute. Relax. Feel a wave of relaxation beginning to move up from your feet now, over the arches and the instep and up to your ankles. A wave of deep, peaceful relaxation moves slowly and consistently up your legs to the calf muscles. For with each breath that you take and with each word that is uttered you experience yourself going deeper and deeper into relaxation.

Your legs are getting very, very heavy and the wave of gentle relaxation moves up over your knees and you are feeling very, very relaxed. The feeling of relaxation moves easily up your thighs, and your thighs are now deeply relaxed. In a moment I will count from one to three and at the count of three, I want you to try to lift one of your legs from the hip. But you will find when you try that the leg has become so relaxed, so heavy, that no matter how hard you try you will not be able to lift the leg, and the harder you try to lift the leg the heavier it will become. And no matter how hard you try to lift it you will not be able to lift it.

One ... your leg is relaxed and heavy and growing heavier and more relaxed by the moment. It is so relaxed that no matter how hard you try to lift it you will be unable to lift your leg ... three, try to raise your leg ... see, you can't, no matter how hard you try, you can't, so stop trying and go deeper, deeper into hypnosis.

Let your entire body settle deeper, deeper down ... down ... down ... your body relaxes into the chair, every muscle relaxing lazily down as you drift deeper, deeper into hypnosis. Your shoulders are relaxed and heavy, your neck, your head go down deeper ... and deeper ... and deeper.

Whenever you choose to count down from eight to one and use the word 'relax' you will become ten times more deeply relaxed than you are now and this is so.

I am going to count the numbers from one to five. At the count of five your eyes will open, your mind will clear and become fully alert, your entire body will be well rested and relaxed, with beautiful feelings moving through the body, and harmonious thoughts in your mind. Here we come ... one ... bring the energy from the sun into your body ... two ... begin moving and stretching, allowing the energy to flow through your fingers and toes ... three, moving, stretching, ... coming up ... up ... up ... four ... almost there ... five, your eyes open, your mind clears and becomes fully alert, your entire body system is well-rested and relaxed.

The exercise can also be practised in bed, lying on your back with the arms alongside the body, palms upwards, visualising a heavy blanket pinning down your legs. If you try to raise your leg at the count of three and succeed in either case, postpone repetition of the exercise until another day. Your analytical mind may require to understand a little more about the need to get out of the way when you choose to use a direct communication procedure.

Initially, there is no need to try to move your legs for more than a few seconds. The object is to encourage the conscious and subconscious levels of mind to accept the same message and function in harmony, not to encourage one level to act against the others. For years, the imitative faculties of the superficial levels of mind have been constantly conditioned, exercised and strengthened at the expense of losing vital access to the deeper subconscious levels. As with an iceberg, the part of mind we are aware of is by far the most insignificant, representing less than ten-per-cent of our total mental potential. We are like those well-meaning people who visit a garden and believe in talking encouragingly to the blossoms when the real trick lies in talking to the roots. Down there is where the real work is done.

Awareness of personal preferences

This is an interesting personal exercise which highlights another aspect of self-hypnosis which can be valuable in ways which are guaranteed to surprise you. Used also by behavourial scientists, the procedure may one day contribute to a reduction in the large percentage of people who fail to find fulfilment in their work. At a purely personal level, what you will learn will greatly increase your overall effectiveness.

The simple requirement is to prepare a shortlist of your personal likes and dislikes as far as the habits, characteristics or personalities of other people are concerned: what do you admire and appreciate in others, what do you dislike or abominate.

You will require a sheet of paper or you may choose to use the fly-leaf of this book. Draw a line down the middle of the page and head the first half 'LIKES' and the second 'DISLIKES'. List only three of each. At a later stage you may find it useful to expand on the initial list. Three likes and dislikes are sufficient to demonstrate the technique: quality of content rather than quantity.

Think carefully of the kind of personality or character you tend to admire and then the kind that you normally would choose to forget.

In three short descriptive sentences, jot down your three preferences, roughly in order of importance to you. Be brief, clear, specific.

Now list in order of impact the three traits that you heartily detest in people. Don't be shy about it, everyone has a right to a personal opinion. Now is an opportunity to state it clearly for yourself, briefly but to the point.

To facilitate later review, the following is provided as an example of the form your comments should take:

'LIKE: People who show appreciation of work well done'.

'DISLIKE: People who only think of themselves'.

Be sure about your choices. The more thought you put into phrasing them clearly, the more benefit you will derive from the subsequent comparison.

If you use a sheet of paper, you may wish to safeguard it or retain it as a bookmark until a later stage. Don't mislay it. Some further exercises are required before we can revert to the subject to see how it can be developed to be of real practical value.

Do the exercise, don't just think about it. You may liken it to a method used in language training or elocution. An excellent way of becoming aware of the improvement in your pronunciation is in listening to your initial recording at a later date. This gives you a boost in confidence which is invaluable in accelerating your continued progress. You will not be disappointed: the better you apply yourself to the task, the better the results.

Stress check. Relax.

Alternative visualisation procedures

Achieving deeper levels of hypnosis is useful in increasing confidence in your capabilities and in quieting the restive mind.

This is a variation in visualising the numbers from eight to one in the countdown procedure. Having centered, use your imagination to see yourself descending in a lift or elevator and passing each floor from eight to ground floor zero. See the descending numerals illuminated in turn as the lift descends without interruption. Each time a lower floor is reached, see the floor number flash brightly.

A further alternative is to visualise the numerals flashing momentarily on a white screen, as though you were witnessing the end-of-reel coding on a film. You may find that you can make them appear alternatively as red and black and you can bring them close to your face or make them recede into the distance.

If the numbers are, at best, vague and indistinct, relax, count down without visualising and affirm: *"With each breath that I take I will go deeper .. deeper ... deeper into relaxation and I will visualise the numbers eight to one .. zero. Now: counting down ..."* and relax as you count. The subconscious mind does not respond to pressure.

Unusual stress, excitement, distractions or the mind-dulling effects of even small quantities of drugs or alcohol will make it necessary to repeat the countdown techniques several times to reach a satisfactory level of relaxation.

The extent to which you can visualise the colours of the rainbow.. red, orange, yellow, green, blue, indigo, violet .. separately or in association with well-known things or places, is another useful test of the degree to which your subconscious is awakening to the new stimulus.

Mood-changing routines

Aim to set aside a specific time for reviewing and practising the various induction tests until you decide which works best for you. This way you establish a new pattern of behaviour which initially facilitates the acceptance of the suggestions. Take as much time as you need. When you are only moderately satisfied with results, you will probably have reached a stage at which post-hypnotic affirmations will be fully effective. Like a trainee pilot who has soloed after a few hours dual-flying instruction, you have taken the first and the most adventurous step in the process that earns you your wings. From here on it is only a matter of gaining more experience, and understanding a little more about controlling the functioning of the hitherto unconscious mechanism of mind.

Make no mistake: we truly make our own luck. More precisely expressed, our individual and collective destiny is largely in our own hands. The more we learn to stand on our own feet, the stronger our legs become. If the thought that we are alone responsible for our destiny bothers you, at least accept that this is how you are choosing to feel, based on your past conditioning. Defer judgment until you experience the reality for yourself. If old beliefs are sound, they will even stand the test of ridicule.

Stress check. Now and then you will be reminded to do this. Check your jaw area. Was it tensed? Tense it consciously and relax it. Now do the same with the cheeks, forehead, neck, shoulders, arms, hands, stomach, thighs, legs, feet, toes. Stretch the arms aloft, inhale deeply, exhale, relax.

Stress check occasionally until such time as you learn not to waste energy in unconsciously tensing the body. You will notice a marked improvement in your reflex actions when they are called into play.

Here are two rapid mood-changing techniques from complementary disciplines. The first requires your response to a simple question: how do you breathe? What is the normal breathing cycle? You breathe in, you breathe out, right? It's a two-cycle movement which you have been doing, more or less unconsciously, for as long as you can remember. It is the same as moving one of your hands from left to right in front of your face, a two-cycle movement, left, then right. Do this now and count the stages. You will have spotted that, in fact, it is four-stage cycle, because there is an essential pause at each end. The same applies to the breathing cycle, 'the movement' originates in the 'nothing' at each end. And emotions come from the same 'nothing' and they are linked to breathing, so whatever our negative emotion is at any time, you can change it to a positive emotion by understanding the interrelationship. Slightly increase or decrease the duration of the pause for a few breaths. That's all. Next time you feel inattentive, bored, tense, tired, irritated, lonely or are subject to any other negative emotion, remember to alter the breathing rhythm slightly.

Why does it work? Negative thoughts and emotions are low vibrational states of mind, like the base notes on a piano. Understanding is a high vibration akin to love. With understanding, all negatives are automatically transmuted to positive influences. This is a universal law. You will find that it always works for you.

If you find yourself indulging in deep depression and other forms of self-pity, there is another technique which is worth testing. It relies on the fact that severe negative emotions cause tension around the jawline and also tend to stiffen the tiny muscles which control the movement of the eyes. Just let the jaw sag loosely and move it slowly, with a circular movement, in a clockwise direction, right to left. Simultaneously, open the eyes as widely as possible and rotate the eyeballs anti-clockwise, slowly and thoughtfully. If you still feel depressed, do the exercise in front of a mirror.

Two forms of therapy are always available to everybody. Silence is the best because it is an open, neutral state of mind, but it is extremely difficult to achieve, because thoughts continue to intrude. Thoughts are energy waves or things which have either a positive or a negative charge or impact. The force of thought is measurable with bio-feedback equipment and a hypnotist has several ways of demonstrating that every thought produces a force field which is tangible and has a clearly positive or negative influence: it attracts or repels. The negative influences always yield to spontaneous laughter, and this is the second-best therapy available to everyone. Laughter that can be shared. Not laughing at somebody else, but laughing with them. Or better still, laughing at ourselves. As understanding grows you will find that we have much more to laugh at and even more to forgive. It helps to remember that angels fly because they learn to take themselves lightly.

What is mind?

"The mind is its own place and in itself can make a heaven of hell and a hell of heaven." (John Milton 1608-1674).

Sigmund Freud, in his day, identified three distinct layers of mind, the conscious, subconscious and unconscious. Around 500BC, the twenty-fifth Buddha, Gotama Siddharta, identified seven. The fourth he referred to as the collective unconscious, which modern psychologists now recognise. This is the level at which telepathy functions, and it is the level responsible for what we term the herd instinct in humans and other living creatures. When a crowd responds simultaneously to the stimulus of a sound or sight, a flock of birds weaves together in the sky or a shoal of fish wheels and dives as one, this is the group mind in action.

An experienced hypnotist can demonstrate fifty distinct levels of consciousness and is aware that there may be finer subdivisions. The Prabaddha Katyyayam identifies seven hundred levels. There is no great significance in the numbers other than to realise that there is always much more to learn. At the conscious or superficial levels of mind which operate on a strictly linear basis, moving from one point to another, it is essential to focus on 'different' aspects in order to achieve some conception of the whole. This can result in misconceptions if we forget that all aspects of body, mind, spirit and environment are one. The same problem can also arise because we arbitrarily assign the labels 'mind' and 'spirit' to what is, in fact, a single unified intelligent energy which permeates and animates every minute living cell and the space 'inside' and 'outside' it, the space from which the vibrations we identify as 'solid' are manifested.

Stress check and relax. The going gets easier from now on.

It is now generally accepted that every living cell is an inter-dependent intelligence responsive to positive and negative signals, apparently electro-magnetic in nature. The positive force of understanding can therefore be directed to modify or eliminate negative bias in and around the body-mind-spirit system and at long-range by using specific focusing techniques.

This poses the question as to which 'part' or function of the mind is capable of waking itself up to the need for taking corrective preventative measures against negative influences. Most of us can accept that we have been subject to conditioning since birth and that our mind is a storehouse of impressions and opinions which the conscious mind has conveyed to the deeper levels as being relevant to our wellbeing or survival. If we are healthy and successful, we can consider that the conscious mind has performed as it should. Otherwise, we can perhaps more readily understand why some Eastern religions identify the intellectual or socially evolved mind as a disease. The word 'devi' is the Hindu word for the conscious mind from which the word 'devil' originally derived. It has scores of other labels, all of them apt. They include programmed, mortal, superficial, social, phenomenal, egotistical, grasshopper and monkey. It is the function of mind that we accept as closest to the five physical senses which serve to maintain a degree of contact with our immediate environment. Yet it is unlikely to be the part of the mind which awakens to realisation of its own shortcomings any more than we could expect an eye to be able to see itself. So at least we can recognise one of the things which the aware mind is not. At the conscious, intellectual level, this is one of the ways we can back into a problem and eliminate some of the possibilities.

Alternatively, in a meditative or hypnotic state, we attain a level of consciousness which is referred to as the witness state. Pathfinder mind is another term which is fairly illustrative as long as we appreciate that the pathfinder is also the path. Accepting consciously that this is the part of mind which has existed in us from the beginning, and which has now awakened to the need to play a less passive role in our lives, is sufficient for most people and most purposes. At some later date you may find it rewarding to catch the feeling of the seed mind at work.

Should you feel an urge to get closer, relax, centre and ponder the story of a famous Zen master who explained to his contemporaries that, during the night, he dreamt that he was a butterfly. His problem was that he was unsure whether he was a man who had dreamt he was a butterfly, or whether he was really a butterfly dreaming that he was a man. Then ponder Shakespeare's comment that a man in his time plays many parts.

They can both point you to a deeper understanding of the witness state of mind, not because the concepts they express are correct, but because the first is incomplete and the second is imprecise and consequently misleading.

> *"To expect us to feel 'humble' in the presence of astronomical dimensions merely because they are big, is a kind of cosmic snobbery.. what is significant is mind."*
> ('Belief and Action', by Lord Samuel)

Post-hypnotic affirmations

Whenever you choose to relax and enter a light state of hypnosis, you can convey suggestions or affirmations directly to the subconscious mind. An example of an affirmation is as follows:

"Whenever I choose to count down from eight to one .. zero, I will enter this level of relaxation and immediately go ten times deeper. From now on water is my favourite thirst quencher, and I will reduce my consumption of all other beverages by half. I desire this and it is so".

Then exit from hypnosis by counting from one to five. You could be more specific as to the quantity and type of beverage you desire to drink daily. Where possible, affirmations require mental statements of fact. If the statement indicates immediacy as illustrated above or is expressed in the present tense, it is understood clearly and accepted at all levels of consciousness. A specific future time, date or event may be given if this is unavoidable.

At the executive levels of consciousness, statements like 'I will try to stop smoking today' are seen for what they are. 'I will try' telegraphs awareness of opposition and the anticipation of possible failure.

Even at the conscious level, when it is pointed out, we can clearly see the difference in self-assurance between 'I will try to stop smoking' and 'As of now, I am a non-smoker'. And whenever you make an affirmation, remember that this is the captain speaking.

The affirmation, coupled with the receptive state of mind, is all that is required to decrease your reliance on chemical and other temporary stimulants. This does not mean that you cannot choose to drink alcohol or tea and coffee from time to time, but two things happen. You are released from attachment to stimulants and you become fully conscious of what you trade for over-indulgence. You trade much more than you think.

If you wish to break an addiction to stimulants of any kind, you will require to prepare an affirmation specifying a daily reduction in intake and add:

"All bodily cells, glands, nerves and other functions are now resuming full normal operations to compensate for the reduction in intake of unnatural stimulants and to restore all systems to full health and vitality."

This statement is required to ensure that the subconscious controls are not only reset to reduce desire for the stimulants, but that the production of natural pain-killing and immunisation fluids is restored to avoid withdrawal symptoms.

Alcohol and other drugs and stimulants interfere with the natural body chemistry, exposing the subject to health problems which would normally be easily avoided. The unnatural chemicals can create an imbalance in the delicate cellular structures which, in turn, results in ill-health and disease.

Minor mental barriers are occasionally encountered with people who place a negative interpretation on counting down to zero. The negative reaction to descending may stem from the misconception that heaven and hell are geographical locations rather than states of mind. Counting down leads to a state of completion, where there is nothing logically left for the conscious mind to do other than to retire to zero. The group subconscious aspect of mind comfortably relates to the ancient significance of the symbol '0' as an indication of the absence of form and mass, denoting absolute freedom from all limitations. As with the 'lazy eight' symbol for infinity, it is a means of overriding our verbal limitations in expressing the inexpressible.

Rules for preparing affirmations

- Identify the problem you intend to eliminate clearly as a basis for the affirmation.

- Word all suggestions or affirmations with emphasis on the specific result required, not the symptoms you wish to remove. Be positive.

- Be brief. The key idea may be repeated in two or three ways to ensure it is understood. Normally limit the number of sentences to seven or eight. Wording should be simple and phrases should be rhythmical.

- Never give yourself suggestions that you do not want to be fully effective. Don't play games.

- Condition your mind to accept the suggestion before you enter self-hypnosis by writing and then reading your suggestion over many times. Take time to improve the clarity.

- As you convey the affirmation, use your imagination to visualise the successful outcome and KNOW THAT IT HAS BEEN ACCOMPLISHED.

Specific examples of affirmations will be given later and these, together with the above rules, will enable you to prepare whatever personal affirmations you may require.

Imagination and desire

Our imagination is usually stronger than we think. Expressed more precisely, our imagination is much stronger than we are capable of thinking. For example, you can wish upon a star for as long as you like, but your dreams have no chance of coming true if your imagination is working against you. No matter how strong your desires, how insistent and fervent your prayers, you will always lose out if they conflict with your imagination. Desire and imagination must work hand in hand and when they do, anything worthwhile is possible.

To illustrate the point, which is a vital one, let us suppose that you have occasion to visit a building-site in winter, when the whole ground area, thanks to rain and heavy traffic, is a sea of churned up mud. Some considerate person has placed a hefty plank en route to the office you need to visit. Without hesitation, you walk along the plank without thinking twice about it. Supposing, however, that an identical hefty plank spans a space between two areas which you require to inspect and there is a sixty foot drop to the floor below. Do you step across the plank with the same confidence? Your desire to do so may be strong, but if the picture you carry in your subconscious mind is of falling ... falling ... and this is dominant, your imagination overrules your desire and you decide not to walk across.

We can upgrade the drama to picture a young girl at one end of the plank, ten storeys high, connecting two apartment buildings. The building and the room in which the girl stands are on fire and the plank represents her only way to safety. Yet she hesitates, her imagination carrying a stronger picture of the danger of falling than of succumbing to fumes and flames. She will have to be coaxed across or driven by pain.

Unreasoned fears and phobias can be much more subtle than this. They can be deeply buried in the subconscious and can repeatedly frustrate our best endeavours and most ardent desires. No conscious effort on our part can override the power of the imagination if it has been conditioned by fear, superstition, hate, envy, worry, jealousy, anger, resentment and any of a host of other negative, self-limiting emotions.

We only have to become aware of the destructive nature of much of what we say and think to see the wisdom of avoiding comments like 'I can always remember faces, but I can never remember names'. With understanding, you learn to identify negative influences and avoid absorbing or internalising them. There may well be as many negative influences in life as there are positive: observe them, accept that they exist, but realise that you do not have to entertain them.

An ancient Zen master expressed this point as follows:
*'That the birds of worry fly over your head, this you must
accept. That they build nests in your hair, this you need not
permit.'*

We can truly be our own worst enemy. Check the following
statements for negative conditioning:

- Whenever I go to a party I drink too much and always
  make a fool of myself.
- I never do well in interviews.
- Money has never been important to me.
- I suppose I will go bald. My father did.
- I always get colds in winter.
- I suppose smoking is bad for me. I'll try to give it up again.

Awareness of negativity is all that is required to avoid it
becoming lodged in the subconscious as a conviction, as part
of your reality. You need to be alert to the negative thoughts
of others. Did you spot the seven negative statements in the
preceding paragraph?

You know the taste of sour grapes and you need nobody
to tell you to spit them out. Do the same when you taste
sour negatives.

So what do you do about the storehouse of self-defeating,
self-destructive influences which have already seeded themselves like pernicious weeds in your being? How do you cast
out the mental parasites before they cloud your whole outlook to the extent that you only feel comfortable with others
who share your negative views? You are already halfway
there: you know where all influences, positive and negative,
are lodged and all you need to know is how to get there.
Coaxing your imagination to join the team is a necessary
first step and this is the purpose of the next exercise.

A famous Mexican master, Genaro, once explained it to
me this way:

*"You are seeking to catch an exceptional fish. Such fish
are not found in a shallow pool."*

Hypnotic induction procedure 'D'

If you have faithfully completed the three earlier exercises and feel unhappy with your responses, there is no cause for concern. One of the monkey mind's favourite ploys is to make us set targets which it then makes sure we will never reach. As the tides ebb and flow, so do the levels of receptivity. Just relax and catch the next high tide.

The exercise again calls for the assistance of a fellow pilgrim with whom you can switch the roles of listener and reader, or better still, record the induction and play it back at a time when you are unlikely to be disturbed. Familiarise yourself with the text, but remember that merely reading and evaluating the suggestions intellectually is worthless in learning to go beyond the superficial levels of mind, which can only see through their past conditioning.

As in the earlier exercises, the suggestions should be conveyed in a normal tone of voice, unhurried and relaxed. Use one of the simple hypnotic techniques to relax you before you start recording. If you miss a word or fluff a sentence, make the correction in a relaxed manner and carry on. Naturalness in conveying the message is more important than mere technical expertise.

This is a Barrie Konicov induction method and it is featured in many of his taped programmes. Should you choose to record the induction, start with the following caution:

"As this is a self-hypnotic recording, it must never be played while driving or at any other time when you require to maintain full awakening consciousness."

Pause and then continue as follows:

"Find yourself seated in a comfortable position, feet firmly on the floor, back straight, hands open and palms resting upwards on your lap. Begin by taking a long, slow, deep breath through the nose. Allow your eyes to close normally and naturally, hold the breath for the mental count of four. Open your mouth and exhale all the breath from your body in a long, low, deep sigh, then let go ... let go.

"*Imagine with me that you find yourself out in nature. I'd like to suggest that you create a magnificent day, that you place yourself perhaps on a beautiful beach, a grassy knoll, a mountain-top, or you may prefer a desert, but wherever you choose, I want you out in nature. Create it as a warm spring or summer day, with a brilliant sun directly above you, a blue sky ... and then put in one or two clouds, light and fluffy, just visible on the horizon. Imagine if you will, the sensation of a gentle breeze blowing from time to time across your body. Are you aware of the smells? Are you aware of the sounds appropriate to the scene you have created?*

"*Now I want you to know that, in the event of an emergency experience while listening to this message, you will automatically come to full awakening consciousness and regardless of the nature of the emergency, you will respond to it in a relaxed, calm and competent manner.*

"*Take a second long, slow, deep breath now, and hold it. Open your mouth and exhale slowly all the air from your body as you mentally count from eight to one and let go. Relax now ... let go. Let go.*

"*Now I want you to know and accept that anytime during this hypnotic experience or any other, whether through the use of a recording or by the direction of a hypnotist or otherwise, you may always bring yourself to full awakening consciousness merely by counting the numbers from one to five. At the count of five your eyes will open, your mind will clear and then become alert, your entire body will be well rested and relaxed, with beautiful feelings moving through your body and harmonious thoughts in your mind.*

"*Now in your mind, in your imagination, focus the brilliant light from the sun over your right arm as you would a flashlight, moving it gently back and forth from the tips of your fingers to your shoulder until you experience the sensation of warmth penetrating the skin, and then the muscles, the nerves, the bones ... until the light of the sun touches every nerve, every cell, every sinew, every consciousness in your right arm. And you find your right arm relaxing and you find yourself drifting deeper and deeper into a gentle state of relaxation, drifting deeper and deeper ...*

"Move the light now, gently, to the left arm. From the tips of the fingers to the shoulders, just move it back and forth until you can sense and experience the warmth from the sun penetrating through the skin and the muscles and the nerves, until both the right and left arm become very deeply relaxed, deeply relaxed, easily, effortlessly.

"Move the light from the sun down the right leg. From the tips of the toes all the way to the big hip joint, the light will focus and move and the right leg goes deeply, deeply relaxed. For with each word that is uttered and with each breath that you take, this feeling and sensation of letting go and relaxing increases moment by moment, breath by breath.

"Focus the light from the sun now over the left leg, from the toes to the hip, back and forth, up and down, deeper, deeper.

"Move the light now, and bring it into the stomach. Focus it there like a radiant ball of energy and feel it beginning to warm and to glow and to sooth every organ, every system, every cell, every atom, every consciousness in your body, and just release, relax and let go and go deeper, deeper and still deeper.

"Bring the light now, bring it up and focus it in your chest and experience the light from the sun entering your bloodstream and feel and sense and know that the energy, the vitality, the life, the light, the love from the sun is surging throughout your entire body, through your bloodstream — to heal, to soothe, to revitalise, as you go deeper and deeper and still deeper.

"Bring the light from the sun now in through your head, and gently move it down your spine until it touches the base of the spine. When it touches the base of the spine it will light up your entire body like a fluorescent light bulb, from the base of the spine to the top of your head and then the light begins to move and to shimmer and radiate ... radiate ... radiate through every nerve of your body.

"You are aware of the energy from the light moving ... moving down and around the pelvic area and down your legs,

*from the small of your back to your stomach, ... from
between your shoulders, around your lungs and your heart ...
across your shoulders and your neck and your head, your
entire body is relaxing more and more. Your shoulders relax,
as does the neck. Your scalp relaxes. The right and the left
lobes of your brain relax. Your forehead, the little muscles
around your eyes, your cheeks relax, your jaw relaxes and
opens slightly and finding saliva in your mouth you merely
swallow it and go deeper, deeper, and still deeper. And
although you are deeply relaxed, as I now count the numbers
from eight to one, you will go ten times more deeply relaxed
on each and every descending number ... eight ... down ...
down ... down ... seven .. six .. five .. four .. three .. two .. one ..
zero .. zero .. zero.*

"Peace and letting go. Each and every time you wish to be
hypnotised you will find that you are able to enter into
hypnosis much more quickly and much more deeply than the
time before. You will find that you can place yourself into a
comfortable state of self-hypnosis merely by repeating
mentally, 'I am going to hypnotise myself for the next fifteen
minutes' or whatever time you choose. Then you will inhale
deeply through the nose, hold the breath to the mental count
of four, and as you exhale all the air from your body, you will
mentally count down from eight to one, zero, and you will
drop deeply into a state of self-hypnosis for the length of time
chosen.

"You will now hear me count the numbers one to five. At
the count of five, your eyes are to open, your mind is to clear
and then become alert, your entire body will be well rested
and relaxed, with beautiful feelings moving through your
body and with harmonious thoughts in your mind.

"Here we come. One .. bring the energy from the sun into
the body again .. two .. begin moving and stretching your
fingers and your toes, allowing the energy to flow and exit
through the fingers and toes ... feel it flow .. three .. moving,
stretching .. stretching .. coming up .. up .. up .. four .. almost
there .. five, your eyes are open, your mind is clearing and
becoming alert, your entire body is well rested and relaxed."

A useful deepening technique to use for brief periods of relaxation or prior to going to sleep at night is to affirm as follows:

"At the count of three, my eyes will open and will immediately close again and I will become more and more relaxed ... counting one .. two .. three .. (eyes open, close automatically) .. going deeper .. 8 .. 7 .. 6 .. 5 .. deeper .. down .. down .. 4 . 3 . 2 .. 1 .. zero .. zero .. zero. Next time I count down from eight to one I will go ten times more deeply relaxed."

The statement about relaxing deeper on the next occasion, expressed as a fact, automatically establishes a conditioned response whenever the countdown procedure is used, eventually enabling you to open the channel to an appropriate level of consciousness in a matter of seconds. You can then direct positive energy to any part of the body you 'put your mind on'.

Of the millions of people who are today awakening to the inborn resources available to them through understanding the mechanism of mind, many only learn when they turn to self-hypnosis as a last resort. They are rarely disappointed, but how much wiser it seems not to need the spur of desperation and to take the time, not only to improve your personal situation as it stands, but to develop invaluable skills in dealing with whatever human drama you may later encounter in life.

Self-reliance and confidence come with experience and with understanding some of the psychological influences involved. It helps to be able to identify some of the interesting landmarks you will pass along the way.

There is a vast difference, for instance, between voluntary and compulsive attention to events. At the deeper levels of consciousness, from your centre of calm, you will cease to allow yourself to be upset by the minor events which irritated you in the past. You will no longer find that you react compulsively with a sense of righteous indignation arising from false pride and fuelled by repressed resentment.

Learn not to resent those who mock and try to irritate and upset you. Feel compassion for them: this is how you 'turn the other cheek'. Perhaps as you yourself were, they are prone to lose themselves in their emotions, anything rather than face the true reasons for their bitterness. Be patient. Whether we realise it or not, each of us is seeking to move along an evolutionary path which has darkness and ignorance at one end and the light of true understanding at the other. We are all pilgrims, some carrying heavier subconscious burdens than others.

As cadet Zen master Camac II expressed it, "I wish I had known all this before I was born". Would it then have been all that much fun just reading about the kind of ridiculous hassles we get ourselves into? Would you believe it possible unless it had all actually happened to you?

The hypnotic state which leads to expanded consciousness requires cultivation of a sensitivity which earlier experiences in life will have tended to dull. Due to our frenetic urges for instant results — levitating now, praying later — we become heavy-handed in our attempts to accelerate progress and this is self-defeating in the extreme. The effect would be similar to pulling up a young plant every day to encourage it to grow. The seed has ben planted and the seed will do the rest. Stress check and relax.

The power of autosuggestion

"He was a simple soul who had never been properly introduced to his subconscious." (Warwick Deeping, 1877-1950).

Through autosuggestion we trigger the response mechanisms which are reached at the deeper levels of consciousness. Under light hypnosis, when you suggest that you will find a dryness in your throat and that you will have an urge to swallow, the resulting throat action is a conditioned response, not a consciously controlled one. You may recall experiencing the confusion of stumbling on a step when you unwittingly allowed the nervous conscious mind to interfere with the automatic step-mounting capability of the subconscious. Once a message is understood and accepted by the subconscious, it becomes entirely routine and self-governing. It passes completely out of the range of control by direct conscious instructions or effort.

How many stress checks have you made without the need for written reminders? There is no need for them now. You can advise the subconscious, under hypnosis, to relax all body tensions when you are reading or writing, and to alert you to those occasions when tensing muscles is a waste of energy, better applied to focusing attention on what you are doing at the time.

Autosuggestion is where the exercises in visualisation and fine-tuning your imaginative faculties start to pay dividends. Until you have experienced the beneficial effect a few times, your intellect may continue to intrude by creating doubts that such a simple procedure can be so amazingly effective. It will eventually accept that it can be a more valuable watch-dog if it ceases to bark at its own shadow.

Autosuggestion differs fundamentally from the usual concepts of prayer. By using imagination, you see and feel that the desired result is already realised. You sense that it is already so, already part of your reality. Where other people and events are involved, the precise means of achieving the desired result are not your concern. To the extent that specific

action on your part is required, you will be clearly and automatically alerted. Your function is to pass the requirement
to the infinite intelligence within your subconscious mind,
which requires nothing more than a clear picture of the desired end result.

Though the subconscious can relate to the conscious level's
concept of time when required to do so, it knows only an
infinite, eternally unfolding moment of 'now'. Consequently
some responses are immediate, as though the requirement
which, in normal terms, would take weeks or even months
to be realised, was in fact an option that was eagerly waiting
to be called into play.

No matter what your situation appears to be at the superficial levels of reality, sense that the control mind has already
responded and that beneficial and corrective measures are
already fully effective.

Have you ever suffered the feeling that you had lost a
wallet or purse full of money and then suddenly found that
it was quite safe all the time? That is the kind of deep-down
feeling of relief you need to encourage. Whether your problem
involves health, finance, employment or any other matter,
visualise the happy solution: see it, feel it, be there ... and
relax. The more you can relax with self-hypnosis, the easier
you will find it is to create the required mental atmosphere.

Love and hate are the two most powerful emotions which
influence Man, but the terms have become vague and insipid
through misunderstanding and misuse. It can be more correct
to define the most destructive negative emotion as repressed
resentment. And nothing available to Man is more powerful
than the positive energy of desire linked to imagination and
deep understanding. When these three positive elements work
in harmony with the natural evolutionary forces which en-
velop and permeate each of us, when we move into tune
with the cosmic flow, no opposition can endure.

Like every other force which Man is empowered to direct,
this immense power of mind can be used for personal advantage without due regard for natural laws or the well-being
of others. As current and past history records, the individual

"My son........even I find it hard to love people I don't even like."

who abuses this power exposes himself to a terrible correction, not in some possible future spiritual existence, but in
his lifetime.

Use the power, use it well, with due regard and compassion
for others. There is no place for suffering or want in Nature.
Vibrant good health and financial abundance are yours as a
birthright. Claim them: the only sin is ignorance, ignorance
of your own unlimited potential for contributing to the joyous
celebration and the incredible cosmic dance that we call life.

For there is a resonance which is renewed from moment to
moment which unites and integrates all things great and
small, visible and invisible. Open to this resonance, flow
with it and and you again become part of the consciousness
of life.

Born as an eagle, why choose to live like a parrot with
clipped wings?

Always seek competent professional advice if you are in
any doubt as to the precise nature of an illness. A
professional will be able to discuss intelligently the
contribution self-hypnosis can make in your particular case.
Never lose your common sense. There is a world of
difference between fooling yourself and developing self-
hypnotic skills to the extent that you are not only entirely
self-sufficient, but capable of channelling healing energies to
other people. Even when you reach this stage, avoid making
health decisions for someone else unless you are also
medically qualified to do so. The 'double diagnosis'
technique which expert hypnotherapists use requires
practical training and years of experience in seeing beyond
the symptoms to the cause, to the negative thought patterns.

Religious beliefs and hypnotism

"And the Lord God caused a deep sleep to fall upon Adam, and he slept ..." (The Christian Bible: Genesis)

Repeating the cautionary note given in the preceding chapter, be sure to pass the responsibility for diagnosing a persistent medical problem to a competent professional. This caution and the warning not to make health-care decisions for your children or anyone else is given clearly and specifically by Mrs Mary Baker Eddy, the founder of Christian Science, yet it is often ignored by people who claim to follow her teachings. Oddly, of the two hundred and thirty commercialised religions, Christian Science is the only one which expresses an official negative opinion of hypnosis. Oddly, because Mrs. Eddy's teachings were derived from what she had learned as a pupil of Dr. Phineas Parkhurst Quimby, a truly remarkable man, a devout Christian.

In his medical practice, Dr. Quimby used psychoanalysis, hypnosis and his unusual skills as a clairvoyant linked to a deep understanding of Hermetic principles. Of Dr. Quimby, Mrs. Eddy is reported as saying: "Nobody has healed like this man since Christ".

The Hermetic principles of the universe were conceived by Hermes Trismegistus, the 'Master of Masters', whose pupils included Abraham, the wise man of the Bible and the original Essenes, the 'Keepers of the Light'. John the Baptist was taught by the Essenes, who also selected and tutored the Messianic Masters from childhood. Anyone who cares to study the Hermetic literature, which survives to this day, will find the source of the spiritual teachings which Masters of all times and nations have always sought to convey. What appear to be contradictory spiritual themes can then be clearly recognised as devices used by individual Masters to jolt people from their customary negatively conditioned concepts of life. These devices were suitable to the times and to the state of understanding and development of the particular people and are meaningless today without an understanding of the tribal fears and superstitions they were designed to supplant.

49

"What say we evolve into two land creatures, you know....with legs and all? You can be first......"

"The religion of one age", wrote R.W. Emerson in 1829, "is the literary entertainment of the next". Khwaja Salahudin, a famous Sufi master, earlier expressed a similar thought: "All religious presentations are variations on one theme, more or less distorted".

In the Christian Bible, there are over thirty references which indicate the masterly use of hypnotic techniques. Deuteronomy 18: 10-11 is the only reference in the scriptures which could possibly be construed as condemning the use of hypnotism, and then only by someone with scant knowledge of the procedure. It goes:

"There shall not be found among you anyone who burns his son or his daughter as an offering, or a charmer, or medium, or a wizard or a necromancer."

The original Hebrew version is more explicit:

"There shall not be found among you any that maketh his son or his daughter to pass through fire, or one that uses divination, a soothsayer, an enchanter, a sorcerer, a charmer, or anyone that consults a ghost of a familiar spirit or a necromancer."

A necromancer is apparently a sorcerer who purports to conjure up spirits of the dead to reveal or influence future events.

Perhaps more than most people, a hypnotist's interest is in helping us to improve the quality of our present lives by increasing awareness of our individual God-given talents. The deeper perception of our links with the past and a clearer vision of future events arise as a natural function of the expanded or enlightened mind, requiring no messages from hallucionary beings or other dubious products of the superstitious and guilt-ridden conditioned mind.

Correcting another biblical quotation to the original version: "Seek that you may find."

It has never been the aim of any true Master to divide man from man. They are not manipulators, charmers or comforters. They provide guidance only to the extent that you can learn to do without them and become responsible in every respect for yourself, not to become an imitator, a follower. Followers can be manipulated easily by exploiting their fears and by promises of future salvation. Repressed resentments can be played upon to the extent that gullible dupes can be encouraged, in the name of religion, to the lunatic, negative extreme of venerating suicide, murder and death.

Self-hypnosis is merely another device, a way of awakening us to our susceptibility to negative, self-destructive programming.

Stay with your present level of understanding if it brings you constant joy and health and a veneration for all forms of life, with frequent bonuses in the form of feelings of immense awe for the natural wonders of this magical universe. Only a masochist need settle for less.

> *"Everything in life is worth living for. Nothing in this world is ever worth dying for".* (F/O Paddy Finucane, DFC, DFM. 1923-42, WW II *Fighter Ace, RAF, Hornchurch*)

Eliminating the negative

"God's first creature, which was light." (Francis Bacon)

There is no need to know, at this stage, precisely how or why the next technique works. Later, you can discover the reasons for yourself. Again, you can be misled by its apparent simplicity. Use it and observe the results. If you have had moderate success with the earlier exercises, this is all that is required.

For illustration purposes, we can consider the case of the common cold, the all-too-common cold. This is one of many afflictions which become rooted in the 'group unconscious'. It is a herd or seasonal belief that you have no way of avoiding becoming a victim in certain well-defined circumstances such as being 'run-down', in the company of others who are suffering, caught in the rain on a cold day and a host of similar seasonal events.

The simple procedure, on first becoming aware that you are exposed to one of your accepted cold-triggering events or even when you first feel the early symptoms of a cold or flu, is to take five. Just take five minutes or less to stress check, centre by breathing deeply, count down and relax. Use whatever visualisation method you prefer to induce mild hypnosis and, at the count of three, bring in the sunlight. Focus it where you have earlier sensed the discomfort and know that the cells will immediately respond. Affirm:

"All functions of my body-mind-spirit system are restored to perfect health and harmony. I desire this and it is so."

Know that your imagination, through the focusing power of your own mind, is now working for you instead of against you.

After you have experienced the effectiveness of this procedure, the thought may occur to you that you may have been mistaken in identifying the symptoms as the beginning of your bi-annual 'flu. So decide to continue to use your imagination constructively and whenever you sense any problem like a cold on the way, just make it seem like another mistake. After a while, even the symptoms will cease to appear.

Your awareness of occasional exposure to all kinds of negative influences and atmospheres will increase. On many occasions you will find that you can simply opt out. For example, there is no need to feel trapped into defending or justifying views and opinions against unduly aggressive minds or people who resort to ridicule to deflect truths they find too uncomfortable to bear. They provide you with an opportunity to bring in the sunlight and direct it from your heart, with understanding and compassion, towards those whose path may be rougher and longer than yours.

A mental spring-cleaning process will be given later together with suggestions for creating a handy safe-house and a positive personal mind shield for all seasons.

Getting to know you

"Our remedies oft in ourselves do lie,
Which we ascribe to heaven." (Shakespeare)

'The Law of Reversed Defects' could be an alternative title for this chapter, because subconsciously we recognise the truth which our conscious awareness hides from: we are seeing our own weaknesses.

At the superficial conscious level we create a false ego, a mirror image of what other equally shallow minds think we are. People who truly love us and see the stupidity in mutual deception or 'stroking', to use the behavioural science term, may attempt to tell us what we truly are, but the message only reaches the conscious mind, which will only accept views which support its own illusions.

We may see fit to modify our behaviour when the boss is around but the personality defect still lies behind the false face worn by the conscious mind. There is good news however, although a shade late for Robert Burns: we all have the power to see ourselves as others truly see us.

To avoid any minor understanding which may develop because we may have been conditioned to read quite different meanings into some common words, let us accept as a definition for love: 'deepest possible human understanding.' Temporary conditions such as sexual attraction, teenage emotions and religious fervour will be so described. The injunction to love your neighbour can then be seen as something more than liking his looks and tolerating his life style. To know what he is really like deep down, all you need to know is what he detests.

This lengthy preamble is partly to camouflage the fact that we are reverting to the exercise you completed on your personal whims and fancies. You can now appreciate that the purpose of the exercise would have been defeated if you had read this section before preparing your personal list and practising relaxation techniques designed to still the conscious mind.

Each dislike is a deeply-ingrained facet of your own

personality which you are incapable — entirely incapable — of accepting consciously, but which you can observe objectively under mild hypnosis.

You will require to rewrite the three statements of dislikes in the form of questions about yourself, for example, 'I hate argumentative people' becomes 'When was I last offensively argumentative? Do I encourage others to express their opinions or do I try to make them wrong? Are my own opinions original? Is there a better way of having a discussion with people?'

After you have changed your negative statements about others to personal questions, ignoring any conscious promptings to spare yourself, induce a comfortable level of hypnosis and ask your subconscious to respond point by point. Later, make a brief private note of what you learn about yourself. Don't expect it to be news to those who truly love you. They have been fruitlessly trying to tell you this for years.

The playful monkey mind will try to revert to old negative habit patterns and invent new ones, but you will spot the attempts and they will eventually decrease. When you see others caught up in similar self-defeating thought patterns, you will be better placed to avoid contributing to their subconscious bias. Unobtrusively and in silence, breathe deeply and bring in the light. When you can do this with deep feelings of love and compassion and no false sense of superiority, at least two of God's creatures will benefit. Accept and be grateful for the experience and watch for one of the final subtle tricks of the role-playing monkey, when you find yourself feeling immensely proud of your humility.

Having exposed your major personality weaknesses you can use the hypnotic questioning procedure to explore minor shortcomings, the 'do I's' and the 'whys'? Do I eat, drink, smoke or talk too much? Why? Do I dislike myself? Find out about yourself. Remember, nobody can tell you: nobody except you. When you see how little you really know about yourself, you can forgive yourself for all your past mistakes. You can learn to know yourself, to like yourself, to live with yourself. You can 'get it all together.' When we are divided in ourselves, we are divided from everybody and everything.

A shield for all seasons

"Nothing in life is so exhilarating as to be shot at without result." (Sir Winston Churchill, 1874-1965)

You will recall that the aim is to offer guidance in using your mental abilities constructively. A difficulty is that our over-stimulated egocentric minds find it difficult to accept that simplicity is the real key to the fullness of life. We unconsciously create most of our problems so that we can busy ourselves trying to resolve them, so stoking and sustaining the false ego-image we present to ourselves and others. By using simple enlightening techniques, you can clean out the mental attic and make it fireproof every morning in less than five minutes. Each time you induce hypnosis you reinforce your ability to access the subconscious control levels and strengthen your protection against the intrusion of negative influences.

Memorise the technique and use it when you have centered and relaxed sufficiently.

Bring the light of the sun down around your body, see and feel it focus on your entire body from above like the beam of a searchlight, until it forms a globe of light, a protective shield if you like or a wall of warm, radiant sunlight all around you. Know that you are protected from all negative influences for the next twenty-four hours and this is so.

You can bring the same radiance into your home or workplace and direct it to people you know with affirmations of 'love, light, life, health, wealth, happiness and fulfilment'.

The mental cleansing process is designed to remove all negative influences which have accumulated from the past or managed to penetrate your guard during the day. You may even be subjected to negative energy emanations while you sleep. You require to visualise a violet flame which you can call forth when you need it. Either tape or memorise the essence of the procedure, which goes as follows:

"You are now deeply relaxed and conscious of a violet transmuting flame rising up all around you and embracing every atom, every molecule, every cell of your body and every

function of your being recognises and knows how to respond positively to the transmuting flame. You can sense and feel the purifying action of the violet flame as it transmutes all negative influences ... NOW." Dismiss the flame with thanks.

At the same time as you mentally articulate 'NOW', pinch the tip of the forefinger and thumb of each hand together for emphasis.

To speed the process along the subconscious avenues of mind, the following affirmation should be used from time to time, after bringing to mind any people or events that you feel were responsible for causing you irritation or offence in the recent or distant past:

"All that has offended me I forgive, within and without I forgive, things past, things present, things future I forgive. I am free and they are free too. All things are cleared up between us now and forever. And most of all I forgive myself for setting all these things in motion."

As mentioned earlier, we cannot avoid exposure to all negative influences and still be part of the ongoing scene. We can avoid entertaining them or taking them to heart in the same way that a gardener avoids cultivating weeds.

The visualisation of the violet transmuting flame is a technique deeply seated in the group unconscious. It pre-dates the techniques of the Islamic, Judaic, Christian and Buddhist masters by hundreds of years and brings with it the power of millions of minds open to the consciousness of Oneness. Simple it may be, yet it requires a high degree of openness and sensitivity even to test its influence. Use it positively, with good intent. It will serve you well.

Bringing in the light ensures a healthier atmosphere in your home and place of work, in fact, wherever you happen to be. Learn to do it unobtrusively: radiate by all means, but don't seek to dazzle. If others come to share your understanding, all the better. Many minds make light the work.

"As with mind, so with masters. Masters who are known publicly are the minority. They have failed to keep out of prominence. Attraction to such a master is part of Lesser Understanding." (Rais T., *Sufi*)

If you have a strenuous work or play session ahead of you or a potentially stressful interview or examination, take five minutes to centre and send some radiance ahead to the place and the people involved.

You can use the violet purifying flame technique in a deeply relaxed state to transmute negative emotions one by one: impatience, hate, resentment, fear, jealousy, envy, greed, anger, intolerance, worry, guilt, whatever.

The sun shines for everyone, but make no mistake, many people of immense negative power walk under a heavy cloud. 'Psychic vampires' is a heavy term, but such beings do exist. They can and do grow fat on the vibrant negative forces of greed and hate and fear. You will become more aware of them, they live by exploiting your weaknesses. Keep the shield up, they retreat. Be grateful: there, but for the grace of God, goes your mother's favourite pilgrim, the one with the bright new sunshine halo.

Seven short steps to awareness

1) When you have decided how to spend the next few minutes or hours of your life — working, sleeping, reading, writing, playing, relaxing — and you find that the grasshopper mind is interfering with suggestions that you should be doing something else, relax, choose. Take five and invoke the full centering technique if the interference persists. Don't tolerate interference. After a time, you will find that you can devote yourself fully to whatever you choose to do. Your growing powers of concentration, of being 'in the now', will surprise you.

2) Assume you are faced with a task which you have chosen to regard as boring, unrewarding, but unavoidable. Change your attitude to it by using the four-cycle breathing routine. Then decide to do the job a shade

faster or slower than you normally would and get started. Find a natural rhythmic way of doing it, swing with it. Make a game of it. If you can't find a job you like, invent one.

3) Stress check, relax, before reading on.

4) What is your reality? Call out your name, as loudly, as your present situation permits. Answer 'Yes sir' or Yes madam', whatever is appropriate. 'Are you there?' 'Yes sir'. All there? Or was your mind somewhere else, lost in illusions of the past or the future? Reminiscing or dreaming instead of being? Brushing your teeth and thinking of something else, you're divided. The more you are divided in your mind during the day, the more you sleep divided.

   As Zen master Joshu might have said:
   "When you sit, sit.
   When you walk, walk.
   If you have to wobble, wobble well."

5) Draw a short line and put the symbol for infinity at each end, signifying that the line extends left and right for ever, beginningless and endless. Now write 'PAST' on the left and 'FUTURE' on the right. Assume that the line represents the movement of the conscious mind. Where on the line would you mark 'PRESENT', the instant of 'NOW'?
   Marking out of one hundred, how much of your life is spent in the now?
   During the next hour or so, check to see if your thoughts and actions are in the same place.

6) Review some of the songs you know or like for evidence or immature emotions, self-pity, negative thinking, dependence on others. For example, change 'You are my sunshine, my only sunshine' to 'You are your sunshine and I am mine'! The 'I' in this event, being the original you, the seed mind, not the egotistical imposter.

   "Song: the licensed medium for bawling in public things too silly to be uttered in ordinary speech". (O. Herford).

"Where did you get those big brown eyes and tiny mind?"
(J. Thurber)

7) At the moment of impulse to do something, STOP. Be conscious as you choose. Be fully in the act, make it all that matters to you, now. Or else don't do it: continue doing whatever you were doing before the sudden impulse to change. Otherwise, who is in charge, the monkey or the organ grinder? Soon your impulses will start to come from the totality of your being, not just from the periphery.

Mind over matter and themes that go bump in the night

The theme that mind can dominate matter has led to a great deal of confusion and disappointment over the years and much of the confusion remains. The idea probably originated in the early scientific endeavours to analyse thoughts and things. Had the experts found access to the works of Hermes Trismegistus, the Master of Masters, they could have saved themselves a lot of misdirected effort. Hermes, 'The Thrice Blessed', later deified by the ancient Greeks and the Romans, spelled out in detail what he saw as the laws and principles which govern the universe, at a time when his fellow Egyptians were assessing load factors and man-hours in building the Sphinx.

One of the basic principles is that the phenomenal world, the material world, is a mental construct. Thoughts are things and things are thought forms. Each and every thought is a positive or negative wave or force field, a building block for the universe. Today we can measure the energy generated by thoughts using biofeedback and other electronic equipment.

In latter years scientists have also learned that the atom, of which all matter is composed, is itself a tiny world, a merry dance of seemingly electro-magnetically activated particles. And each sub-atomic particle, in turn, is itself another tiny universe. When the particles are subjected to observation they react like amateur actors, apparently conscious of the fact that they are being observed. They fade and reappear as waves or other kinds of particles. The best scientific description of them to date is that 'they resemble thought forms'.

The Hermetic principle of power, achieved by bringing thought into harmony at all levels, is well illustrated by the spontaneous focusing of thought-energy achieved at a time of compelling need. All channels switch to survival mode and consciousness expands in every nerve, cell and sinew, often resulting in seemingly superhuman action.

My own clan history, stored in a library in Rothesay, Scotland, records that one of my direct ancestors, fighting a lone rearguard action against attack by "a group of marauding Campbells", cleared a chasm with a sixteen-foot backwards leap. What an opportunity this provided for Gaelic enlightenment, probably discarded by clan elders in favour of a crash course in hopscotch, backwards. We can pose the question today: can we stay in this apparently superhuman awareness mode permanently without strain or the need for outside stimulus, such as swords?

At the superficial conscious levels we seem to function as separate physical entities, with such freedom to think and act as our particular social system and circumstances permit. With a little more awareness, however, we can see that we are all interdependent; no man is an island. And islands, in any case, are also interdependent. Without at least sea and space around them they would not be islands. So if we know the social rules and laws and regulations and accept the wisdom of them in maintaining our interdependence, we live to some degree in peace and harmony within our social environment.

At the deeper, vital subconscious levels of mind the rules and principles are perhaps more flexible but, as H. A. Vachell explains, "in nature there are no rewards or punishments, only consequences." For the moment, it will suffice to accept that there is substantial evidence available to anyone who seeks to know that our world, our reality, is a mental construction and that all thoughts are things, positively or negatively charged. Things which are invisible but measurable energy fields or forces, either friendly or unfriendly, never neutral.

Thus our reality, the world we know, is a world of effect, not cause. It causes nothing to happen because it is itself a caused thing. And, as Barrie Konicov explains, "As a professional hypnotist, regardless of the conditions your clients face you with, you will know that the condition is not the cause, but a symptom, because cause is always thought."

Yet, though everything which is manifested in our world, in our level of reality, is a product of mind, of the totality of mind, it is not necessarily an instant product of an individual mind. Our individual thoughts are not, themselves, compelling forces for good or ill. They are building blocks. Placed in harmony with the environment, with 'that which is', both within and without, envisaging, feeling, knowing the perfect realisation of the event we desire, the building process is set in motion. The same incredible process which builds and continuously maintains the mini-cosmos of our being from within only needs to see the blueprint. The more we are attuned to our next greatest good, to 'right action' or the fulfilment of our individual purpose in life, the faster the result.

Each of us is a child of the universe with a right to be here. We are not intruders, isolated from our world. We are of the self-same stuff, we are part and parcel of it all. We have a purpose in being, a role to play in life. You will have glimpses of it from time to time: the opportunities of a bountiful universe await. There is light, love, health and material abundance for everyone. This is our birthright, like the air and the water, it comes with the territory. It waits only to be claimed.

For to be human is not to be puny, dependent or weak. To be human is to be all that there is in the vast fullness and glory of life. And the fullness and glory of life is a magical gift indeed. Open to the magic of it for a while, whirl and dance with it. You will soon find the rhythm again. The dance will lead you to a greater state of being than any marks on paper can ever convey.

Every cell in our being is a minute intelligence, a part of one mind, born of the original seed cell. There is no mind over matter, or matter over mind. The seed energy is never destroyed. It disperses. It expands. It changes its form.

Monkey tricks and the muddle way

"The pendulum of the mind oscillates between sense and nonsense, not between right and wrong." (C.G. Jung).

People who exhort you to have faith and to trust and believe in them, are sadly lacking in a basic understanding of how the human mind works. The duality, the pendulum or yin-yang effect is always there. Say 'trust me' to someone and doubt enters immediately on the same waveband. It has to. Trust and doubt are degrees of the same energy. Trigger one and you trigger the other. You might just as well ask someone to spin one side of a coin.

One moment we trust and the next instant we doubt. And this is how it is with everything the mind identifies as opposites. One minute we laugh and love and the next minute we weep and hate. We bounce from one side of the cage to the other, so conditioned to our monkey-mind antics that we fail to see that the cage has no roof. See how the monkey jumps, become aware of it. Don't struggle with it or try to pin it down, this only encourages it to invent new tricks, even more subtle than the last. Watch, then the unimaginable happens. The pointless activity ceases by itself and a different quality of awareness, understanding and compassion permeates every aspect of your life.

Your centre of control is no longer being bounced perpetually between hell on one side and heaven on the other. Transcending duality, you hop nimbly out of the cage. You never saw it as a cage because you built it yourself and you called it your way of life. You were led to regard your monkey-mind as your most valuable asset. It was also your most pernicious enemy. As a guide and master, a tragic misfit at best. Is it any wonder that most of us can be replaced by machines?

Stress check. Shoulders, neck and the rest. What is the monkey mind up to now? Analysing, wishing, regretting, repenting? Centre, relax, let go.

Before settling down to some interesting specifics, there is a point about mind-matter unity that is worthy of comment. Whether in self-hypnosis or meditation, as consciousness expands and the mental spring-cleaning progresses, you will become aware of unconscious body movements, twitches and 'shruggings off', part of the process of unwinding. Don't be disturbed, be glad to see the repressed tensions go. Later you may come to miss this physical evidence that the mind-body complex is moving into harmony at subtler levels.

The monkey has been masquerading as master for a long time, at least since your childhood. It will play many tricks to maintain its posture as lord and master. 'Revelations' are not an uncommon ploy, often occurring some time after an effective spring-cleaning session. A Buddhist, for example, will see himself sitting under a bodhi tree, hearing great truths from the lips of the Master. A Christian-conditioned mind will be entertained by angels with harps. A Hebrew mind will project a stern, father-figure image of God, or a passable Moses look-alike indicating the way. In Zen terms, this is all 'makyo', abominable illusion, a kind of mirage that the conditioned mind produces to divert attention from reality. The illusion may be repeated with variations at a later date. Each is a fiction with as much validity in terms of spiritual experience as a low-budget pantomine or soap-opera. It can serve a useful purpose by indicating that you are on the right path, but you are pressing forward at a faster pace than your past conditioning can tolerate. Ease up and take time out for a few days. Eternity can wait. The channel is opening and the way ahead will reveal itself to you in its own good time, you can count on that.

There are plenty of well-meaning but insecure people who think that they have to be constantly clever or entertaining to be accepted. In much the same way, the intellectual mind feels that it has to be constantly active, never at rest. Its real function is to check the messages from the senses objectively. This is a fact. Meaning that this is a fact from where I happen to be looking at the moment, so test it for yourself before you reject it or add it to your conditioning. Check by regressing under hypnosis to your birth to see how your thinking has been pressed into a mould. Once you see this, you will automatically check your superficial impressions with the deeper levels of mind and permit only healthy, constructive impressions to be placed in storage. They will need to be taken out and further updated as your understanding develops. Your understanding, that is, of how the mind functions. Life itself is not something we need to understand. It is simply an experience to be enjoyed, with no other purpose than that. When you fully understand the functions of mind you will see that each of us has the power, not only to choose how we live, but to choose for how long: to choose the quantity as well as the quality of life. How it was before this lifetime and what happens next is unimportant and can become another distraction from understanding the ongoing living experience.

André Maurois avoided this needless distraction by the simple application of logic:

"Either the spirit is immortal and we shall not die spiritually, or it perishes and we will never know we are dead. So live, then, as though you were eternal."

"Pull hard down on the left, Baba Ram — and point thy butt more into wind..."

The daily fifteen

"It is better to have loafed and lost than never to have loafed at all." (James Thurber)

Choose a time and a place where you can sit in comfort for fifteen minutes every day, rain or shine, free from interruption. If a child is present, let it play happily while you sit. Let the child join you only if it chooses to do so. Explain what you do but no more. A sleeping baby or child will benefit from your exercise.

Just as you should ensure that at least ten-per-cent of your earnings is yours to save, insist that this fifteen minutes a day is part of your life savings. Make it thirty minutes and you will have more to share.

Don't sleep or doze. Sleep is an escape, avoidance, postponement. Self-hypnosis and meditation are altered states of consciousness, providing a new perspective on life, a new vantage point from which to observe.

Relax, breathe deeply, centre, let go. Focus on your breathing, prolonging the pauses slightly, balancing the four movements. Visualise the inhale-pause-exhale-pause cycle as though the four phases were following the circumference of a circle, a circle extending outwards from the centre of your forehead and returning by way of your stomach. That's it. While you are focusing on your breathing, let thoughts float as they will, and ignore them. Resist any temptation to memorise what is happening, don't follow the thoughts, let them drift by. There will be plenty more.

Revert to focusing on your breathing if the thoughts keep crowding in. They will gradually slow down. Don't try to stop them, you can't. Not yet. See them as clouds, obscuring your view of the heavens. The clouds are temporary, the sky is always there. Don't expect instant miracles; you are planting another seed. A season will come and it will flourish. Then it will blossom.

Fifteen minutes of your life, for yourself, every day. Active loafing, that's all.

To assist them in reaching a deeply meditative state,

aspiring meditators are advised initially to follow a daily routine, so that they become accustomed and attuned to the sounds and the atmosphere of the place in which they choose to meditate. A particular posture, ritual chanting and the burning of incense all contribute to conditioning the restless senses into a state of relaxed acquiescence.

Tranquil surroundings are also important in the introductory stages of practising hypnotic skills and, particularly for feelings-orientated people, some simple physical gestures, appropriate to the mental state, can be helpful. The technique of pressing together the tips of the forefinger and thumb, as you pass suggestions to the subconscious, has a reinforcing effect. Use it to emphasise, 'and this is so' and the 'now' of suggestions as in 'Transmute all negative influences to strong, positive forces, now.'

You may also feel like raising your arms, fingers outstretched, as you count up to the awakened state, feeling the inflow of the cosmic energies which surround and sustain everything in the universe.

Build on these suggestions as you see fit, follow your own star. There is no membership obligation and no call for public display or posturing. As with meditation, self-hypnosis is something which is strictly between you and you.

Awareness and energy flow

This is a variation on the stress check routine.

Place the book where you can still read it, freeing your hands to do the exercise now. Same deal: you will learn from doing it, not just by thinking about it.

Place the hands together at chest level, finger tips pointing upwards to the chin, arms bent at the wrists, elbows spread widely apart. Now press the hands together as tightly as you can, to the limit of comfort.

Which arm is the stronger? Press hard and decide. Then relax and read on.

Normally blessed, we are aware that, in the arm department, we are equipped to the tune of two. This is our awareness at the conscious or surface level. At the deeper levels, from which all things manifest, there is only one energy, taking numerous forms. We can direct this energy in many ways. While sitting, for example, we can press down on our knees, then raise our heels to develop stomach muscles. You need no weights or springs, you can do it all to yourself. Charles Atlas called these dynamic tension exercises. Unconsciously, we fall into the habit of tensing facial, shoulder, neck and scores of other muscles continuously and these are all signs of stress-induced conditioning.

For the same reasons, this is also what we are continuously doing unconsciously at the mental level. We are using the same energy, there is only one. We produce a constant state of mental tension where there are no muscles to develop. We do it all to ourselves, all the time.

Now put the book down again, raise the arms high over your head, stretch upwards and relax.

Feels good, doesn't it?

Now do the same with your mind.

Health and harmony

"In the province of the mind there are no limits."
(Dr J. Cunningham Lilly)

Emile Coué was an eminent hypnotist who originated the well-publicised autosuggestion formula, 'Day by day in every way, I'm getting better and better'. By repeating this phrase daily and particularly before going to sleep, thousands of seemingly hopeless invalids have been cured. Yet consciousness of our bodily existence is still a mystery that science is unable to explain and no man in the world knows the limits of the power available to the human mind. That we have the power to raise our biochemical nature to its original perfect state can be demonstrated and we can learn to channel this power to others. There is no real mystery about this, other than why it takes us so long to learn how to use these God-given assets.

We know that nothing in this world is created by Man. Everything already exists as a latent possibility. By concentrating our attention, some of the infinite possibilities are consciously actualised: we bring them into our reality, we cause them to manifest.

Earlier, to avoid misinterpretation, a definition of 'love' was offered. To avoid any limitations caused by beliefs and disbeliefs, let us accept that the term 'God' refers to the initial letters of the three Greek words for 'that which is', from which the word God was originally derived.

We have become overly identified with our bodies and material things. To a large extent, it is our over-reliance on our limited senses of sight, smell, touch, taste and hearing that causes our difficulties. We allow ourselves to become unduly impressed by size and mass and forget what the invisible atom can do. Bear in mind that, not so long ago, each of us was a tiny group of cells, thousands of which would be needed to fill a thimble.

We can deep-think the point using a less personal example. Reversing an old adage: 'From the mighty oak, tiny acorns grow.' Each tiny acorn provides sustenance both for the unseen intelligence within and to attract a squirrel that chooses to bury the acorn for a future meal and hopefully forgets to collect it. This minute intelligence carries the blueprint for an oak tree and proceeds to manifest it, expanding it from within, roots and all. The most sophisticated computers built cannot match such a trick and yet Nature is so prolific that it can afford to provide every individual acorn, every single seed, every cell, human and otherwise, with this incredible inbuilt intelligence. What then of the microscopic cell or cells that we call mind? What is the effect on them of the physical and mental influences or disturbances in their environment?

As mentioned earlier, hypnotists can demonstrate fifty distinct depths of hypnosis, indicating the different levels of subconscious control, from simple physical relaxation to the catatonic state in which all spontaneous action is inhibited. Suggestions and other 'outside' influences can apparently reach all the subconscious levels, which are also seen to respond to the vibrations of our most dominant patterns of thought. Each cell has its own inbuilt intelligence and an antenna, a two-way interconnection with the functioning of the whole living system. When our consciousness is habitually lost, for example, in regrets for the past and concern for the future, the subconscious levels of mind get out of harmony with the environment and lose touch with the ongoing flow of life. Whatever positive or negative picture-message is conveyed and accepted as true is made manifest at some level, in some form or another. Cells rearrange themselves to respond to the instructions from the medulla. Anything which appears in or on the body can only do so because there is a mental pattern corresponding to it.

The founder of the American Institute of Hypnosis and the first fulltime practitioner of hypnosis in America, William J. Bryan, developed a way of analysing the subconscious mind to show that, by accepting false impressions and limiting thoughts, the mind creates all illnesses.

Cancer cells, for example, are ordinary cells out of balance and control. The whole problem of disease is the confusion and eventual collapse of the organisational wholeness and harmony of our being.

We know that every form of energy is friendly, once we learn how to relate to it correctly. Yet we even grant words the power to stir our deepest emotions so that we can feel elated or hurt. The squirrel we referred to earlier has been known, in some areas, as a tree rat. A common or garden tree rat. Accepting a three letter sound can change our feelings about squirrels, because of what we associate with the word 'rat'.

That ancient Master-Mastermind, Hermes, held the view that the entire natural world is manifested in Man, that he is a microcosmos and like everything else, an essential part of the macrocosmos. Good health, from the Hermetic viewpoint, means that the qualities of all the elements acting in and on the human body, act in harmony.

No reason is seen for permitting such a disharmony in any element that an obvious disharmony like illness or disease should manifest. Genuine good health, in turn, is seen as a normal consequence and evidence of a thorough understanding of universal natural laws which require the elements to perform specific functions, to build, to maintain and to renew.

Once you can understand and fully accept that you are solely and personally responsible for your own life, you can decide to do something about it. Your options would seem to be limited, due to your earlier lack of understanding. This thought would be negative conditioning, which also happens to be the only thing that stands in your way.

As you know, anything you hear or read at the conscious level of mind is either accepted or rejected by reference to past influences or beliefs. We accept what we feel comfortable with, because we have become accustomed to the walls of our cage. This is why attempts at 'positive thinking' or reading about how to improve yourself are as futile as making New Year resolutions. If you want a change of tune, you need to convince the organ grinder, not the monkey.

So when you read some of the succeeding chapters dealing with health and addictions, even if you have freed yourself or have never been trapped, you will find it beneficial to follow the instructions to induce light hypnosis as you read them. Your understanding of those who have fallen unwittingly victim to intense negative conditioning will deepen, as will your compassion. If a close friend or relative is a victim, you will at least learn how to avoid contributing unconsciously to his or her self-destructive illusions.

Ten-minute health session

"Oh isn't life a terrible thing, thank God."

(Dylan Thomas)

As you grow in experience, your subconscious can be relied upon to prompt you to take appropriate action for your health and wellbeing. You will develop natural health intelligence. A brief self-hypnosis session each morning and evening will suffice to keep you in perfect health. Refresh your memory of the rules for forming autosuggestions so that you can be sure they are correctly conveyed, remembering that the positive quality of your thoughts and feelings is important at the time you make them.

The procedure is a condensed version of techniques you have practised. Rehearse your affirmation so that you can enter into it fully: make it real and it is real. As you enter the spirit of the moment you will find that you can improvise, introducing natural flair, style and rhythm, though never at the expense of clarity. If you have any specific needs, include them in the affirmation.

1) Relax, centre, let go.

2) Bring the sunlight in, radiate, form the protective shield.

3) Transmute all negatives in and around the body-mind-spirit system to positives.

4) Affirm: *"Love, light, life, health, wealth, and happiness*

*are mine, to share in harmony with everyone. And this is
so".*

5)   Exit to the count of five, stretch, enjoy.

Self-hypnosis and the smoking habit

As a non-smoker, you will learn from this chapter why your
best efforts to persuade a close friend or loved one to kick the
habit have failed.

If you are a smoker and have a genuine desire to stop, read
on, because you have taken the first essential step already.

Breaking a habit requires more than will-power. It requires
a realisation of what you trade, of what causes it to become a
habit in the first place and of how to drop it now, without
substituting another addiction or suffering withdrawal
symptoms. Being a habit, you know that it has passed out of
control of your conscious mindpower, so appeals are
ineffective, the die is cast. Exercising willpower is like trying
to force your left hand down with your right, you only
succeed in straining both arms. Suppress the habit and it
strengthens the desire. Understand it, it drops. After all, that
is how it started, more or less effortlessly. Right now, one
part of your head enjoys smoking, another part knows that it
hurts.

For the mechanically-minded, there is a way of illustrating
how all habits are formed, for better or for worse. Not too
long ago, torpedoes were relatively simple devices. Their
speed was fixed and there were manually adjusted settings for
depth and direction. Once set and fired, a torpedo normally
travelled at the preset depth and in the direction required. If
the settings were wrong, the torpedo missed. Later versions
could be guided by radio signals, in other words, a way was
found to override and correct the initial settings. The same
applies to habits. There is a way to reset the mental controls

"No I wasn't saying anything. It should stop soon – I gave up smoking last week."

so that you become the puppet master instead of the puppet.

We came into this existence as suckers, all of us. When there was nothing else provided, we sucked our toes or our thumbs, we comforted ourselves that way. Older, wiser, but not mature, we sucked pens and pencils, straws, lollipops and candies. Later, we found childhood comfort in sucking warm smoke and the people who profit from providing the weed convinced us that this is an acceptable social vice for adults. Success and power were identified with sporting a twelve-inch teat-alternative, a Corona-Corona, a highly-priced hand-rolled soother. All of which means nothing to the addict of course because, in every sense of the word, he has been a sucker since birth.

Make a note of today's date or choose a future day and date on which you have decided to stop smoking. Write it at the top of the page now.

You are advised to tape the following message for yourself, to follow on from the induction in which the sun is pictured as shining down and all around you. Alternatively, if you can achieve a satisfactory level of relaxation and mental harmony by using one or several induction techniques, do so now, adding the instruction, *"at the mental count of three, my eyes will open and I will continue to read while maintaining a relaxed state of awareness at all levels of mind."*

I stopped smoking at .... am on .... the ..... day of .... 19.....

The following procedure is designed to reinforce my determination never to smoke again from this date onwards. I am now a non-smoker.

"I take a deep breath and bring the sunlight into my body and I feel it glow and radiate as it enters my mouth and permeates the respiratory system. With each breath that I take I feel the sunlight radiate .... radiate .... radiate in my throat and lungs and all the cells respond, setting in motion the healing process to correct any malfunction that may exist in the mind-body-spirit system. The purifying light enters and I am cleansed, now.

"I wish now to disconnect and remove all mental and physical, emotional and other associations with the practice of smoking. As each possible association is spoken, all connections with it will be severed immediately and permanently from all levels of consciousness.

- *"Any association with the first cigarette of the day, with morning smoking, I reach up in my imagination, disconnect, stop. Stop smoking.*
- *"Any association with driving or being driven in a motor vehicle, I reach up, disconnect, stop. Stop smoking.*
- *"Any association with speaking on the telephone, I reach up, disconnect, stop. Stop smoking.*
- *"Any association with my job, work breaks, I reach up, disconnect, stop. Stop smoking.*
- *"Any association with meals, before, after or during meals, I reach up, disconnect, stop. Stop smoking.*
- *"Any association with decision making, I reach up, disconnect, stop. Stop smoking.*
- *"Any association with social occasions, trying to be one of the gang, I reach up, disconnect, stop. Stop smoking. It's all right for me to choose to stop smoking and still be appreciated as a good friend and companion.*
- *"Any association with household or garden chores, I reach up, disconnect, stop, Stop smoking.*
- *"Any association with glamour or style, I reach up, disconnect, stop. Stop smoking.*
- *"Any association with sporting occasions, parties, watching TV, reading, I reach up, disconnect, stop. Stop smoking.*
- *"Any association with anger, tension, frustration, loneliness, boredom, sadness, I reach up, disconnect, stop. Stop smoking.*
- *"Any association with fear, resentment, nervousness, rejection and any other negative emotional influences, I reach up, disconnect, stop. Stop smoking.*

"I now reach up and disconnect any psychological factors which may be associated with smoking. I am aware that the addiction is recognised as an unconscious death urge and I affirm that my life urge is now ten times stronger than any negative influence, compulsion or urge. I reach up and disconnect all negative compulsions. Stop. Stop smoking. I affirm that I choose to breathe, not to smoke.

- *"If smoking has been associated with any form of oral gratification for me, I disconnect, stop. Stop smoking.*

- *"If at any time in the past smoking has been associated with any form of guilt, I disconnect, stop. Stop smoking.*

- *"If any other associations with smoking remain, let them be clearly identified* NOW ....

I reach up, disconnect, stop. Stop smoking.

"I now relax still deeper and bring the sunshine in, radiating throughout my whole being, eliminating all influences and effects associated with smoking, NOW ....

"With my mind's eye I examine carefully all areas of my lungs and respiratory system .... All tissue, nerves, cells and other bodily functions are now performing as they should in vibrant good health and harmony and this is so.

"I breathe deeply. I am much more relaxed and at ease. As I count down from eight to one I go ten times deeper into relaxation counting eight ... deeper, more and more relaxed ... seven .... six ... five .... drifting, drifting deeper ... four ... three ... two ... one ... zero .. zero .. zero ...

"Each and every suggestion I am about to make is to be fully effective immediately as a total and permanent part of me. Each suggestion is for my benefit, I desire it, truly desire it, and it is so.

"I am in charge of myself and am not misled by my senses. I chose to stop smoking because I wanted to stop, and I did.

"Whenever an impulse arises in the future to indulge in negative habits, I will be reminded to centre my breathing, counting down from eight to one and the negative urge, impulse and desire is to dissolve out of my life, out of all levels of mind immediately. My awareness of negative im-

pulses increases day by day and soon, and very soon indeed, my rejection of self-destructive habits will become automatic and spontaneous and this is so.

"*I have no feeling of anxiety, resentment or irritability because I made a personal decision to quit and I did. I avoided the self-defeating games of thinking about trying to quit, I just stopped. I have no need to substitute other forms of sugar addiction for tobacco leaf. I have a sense of joy, attainment and release. I am no longer a slave to a weed. Cause has been revealed to me and the habit is dissolved.*

"*Day by day my resolve to remain in charge of my life is reinforced and strengthened. Now, in my imagination, I see myself living the next twenty-four hours, freed from the habit of smoking. I'm calm, relaxed and happy — it's a beautiful twenty-four hours. Certainly there may be some rough moments, but I can handle them. I'm a mature person, in charge of my own life, I need no crutches. Now, in my mind's eye, I go seven days ahead. I'm relaxed, healthy, confident in myself. Now I go thirty days ahead, a whole month without props and crutches. I'm free ... happy, healthy, tremendously alive. Life is an incredible experience: it's mine to enjoy.*

"*If this message has been recorded and is being played at your normal bedtime, your subconscious mind is instructed to ignore the awakening instructions and you will continue sleeping soundly until your normal awakening time, when you will wake up feeling fully refreshed and alert, ready to meet another great day of opportunity. If you are playing this message other than at your normal bedtime, you will awaken at the count of five. At the count of five your eyes will open, your mind will become clear and alert and you will awaken feeling fully refreshed, invigorated, very much alive.*

"*One, beginning to come up. Two, beginning to move and stretch. Moving stretching .. three, coming up .. four .. if this recording is being played at your regular bedtime your subconscious mind is voiding these awakening suggestions .. five .. if this recording is being played at other than your regular bedtime you are now fully aware that the number five has been counted and you are coming to full awakening consciousness."*

As a non-smoker, you will find how unpleasant a habit it is when others smoke. Understanding that smoking is a sign of immaturity, a hangover from childhood illusions, you will find that you don't have to prove anything to anyone when you stop. You will find it easy to maintain your integrity and to be true to yourself.

Smoking was never a good idea anyway. It doesn't relieve tension, it only distracts you from seeking the cause. Now you know where and how to seek the cause of any habit. There is infinite intelligence inherent in the development and continuous renewal of the living cells of the body and in the magical energy which activates them. They all respond to your habitual and most dominant thought patterns. You can share with them a clear common aim: their urge is always lifewards. Their aim is to survive in radiant good health.

You may find that some people are your friends only because you complemented their weaknesses, and they now feel uncomfortable because you don't. Are they really the kind of friends you need? When anyone or anything creates a need in you, you lose your freedom, your independence. Hang loose, relax, don't be intimidated or put down by people who lack the sense to see their own childish folly. There's an old Spanish saying that goes: 'Better to be alone than in bad company.'

If you feel that you need to tape the procedure, play the tape through once or twice when you are unlikely to fall asleep and nightly at bedtime for several nights.

You may find that relaxing and making the following affirmation is sufficient:

"I am a non-smoker. I am in sole charge of my health and wellbeing. I treasure above all things the gift of life. I dedicate myself to understanding and to maintaining my body- mind-spirit in love, light, life, fitness and health, in harmony with all, and this is so."

Weight control with self-hypnosis

"The only light in his life comes on when he opens the refrigerator door." (H. Butzky)

Excessive eating is recognised as an acquired habit. Fat, we could perhaps say, is a frontal and side effect. Determine the underlying cause with self-hypnosis and the habit is controlled or eliminated, without any emotional or physical stress, strain or effort. Self-understanding is again the keyword, not self-control. Once the negative thought patterns are recognised, the subconscious levels of mind will be free to maintain your body in perfect shape at whatever weight level is healthy for you. You will find that you no longer need to eat just to give your gut exercise or to feed a hungry head.

Before all meals and whenever you feel the urge to eat, take a long, slow, deep breath, hold it for the mental count of four, exhale through the mouth in a long, low sigh and count down from eight to one. Have available a copy of the following eight points and refer to it until you can memorise the gist of it:

8. I am relaxed totally, mentally and physically.

7. I am losing two to seven pounds in weight monthly until I reach my ideal weight.

6. I am losing weight and feeling great.

5. I eat less and taste food more.

4. I leave food on my plate and feel great about it.

3. I like to feel slightly hungry even after meals.

2. I can visualise myself as I will look when all the excess weight is gone.

1. All these suggestions are a permanent part of me.

Exit from hypnosis to the count of five.

At least once a day, take time out to relax, centre and re-read the suggestions, adding the following affirmation:

"I centre and relax whenever I feel the urge to eat. I drink a pint of water before every meal and throughout the day,

81

whenever I feel tempted to snack. I will not permit negative emotions to trick me into eating. I will be alerted to them and I will find the cause. I choose water as my favourite thirst-quencher. Each time I drink water I reinforce my resolve. Every day in every way I am better and slimmer and more in control of my life and my health. I desire this and it is so."

Consult your medical advisor before taking steps to lose more than a few pounds in weight. He will suggest what precise weight should be your goal. With hypnotic techniques, your body mechanisms will automatically adjust to your ideal weight, but other health factors may require to be considered in starting a serious weight reduction programme.

Studying earlier material, you will have appreciated that appeals to common sense and other attempts to put pressure on the conscious levels of mind are futile in countering an immature or obsessive compulsion to use food as a distraction or substitute for some lack or hurt, imagined or real. Attempts to diet activate the law of reversed effect: increased tension and depression further increase the urge to over-indulge. With self-hypnosis, no futile appeals to will-power are involved, nor do you have to be a martyr or a masochist. Just practise the various relaxation procedures until you find the one that suits you best ... and keep a handy bottle of water available in the refrigerator.

The association-removal suggestions detailed in the preceding chapter can be readily adapted to eliminate the deep-seated cause of your compulsive eating habit simply by changing 'Stop smoking' to 'Stop eating excessively'.

Once you have eliminated the cause, the subconscious does the rest for you. Until then, be alert to the fact that outside every fat person there is an even fatter person waiting to get in.

Robert Quillen devised a practical reducing exercise which has the merit of simplicity. Basically, it involves placing both hands firmly against the edge of the table and pushing back.

Controlling the drinking habit

"Stay on top, man: avoid strong drink.
Drink is what keeps the herd in the low country."
(John D. Rockefeller)

If you are an occasional moderate alcohol drinker, you clearly have no serious problem. Not being habituated to it, you are not subconsciously controlled by it. If you become dependent on it, you have a serious double problem. Firstly, you will be slow to recognise and accept that you have a problem, because alcohol obviously dulls the perception. Secondly, you drink excessively because alcohol provides an escape from your own conception of reality, consequently you will tend to run away from making an essential personal decision. Essential, because unless there still remains enough courage to face up to the fact that you have a problem and you personally resolve to master it, nobody — nobody else — can help you. The addiction will continue to offer what seems like an easy way out. As with drugs, it is a simple way of dulling the senses without immediately harming the body. So you can let matters drift and postpone finding out why you think you need a chemical crutch, at least for as long as your vital organs last. You meanwhile inhabit a twilight world between life and death, an unwitting slave to every illusion that a stupified mind can devise.

The good news is that the law of yin-yang, of polar opposites, operates everywhere. Only those who have been trapped at the lower levels of existence can ever experience the joy and the bliss of shedding their shackles. The strength of the habit itself is clear evidence of the immense power of thought available to apply to the control of the addiction. It can lock you into a habit even though you are aware, at another level of mind, that it is negative and self-destructive.

The curative power of your subconscious mind can never be impaired. It can be freed from the negative thoughts, the sense of inferiority, hurt, shame, guilt, rejection, resentment and anger. The instructions for bringing the unlimited power of mind to your aid are similar to those for eliminating the tobacco addiction. They can be adapted as necessary, bringing in the light, in your imagination, to heal and replace the nerves, cells and tissue which have been impaired.

Because of the double problem in self-treating drinking and drugs, a later chapter will offer an alternative approach. Meanwhile, develop confidence in the simple hypnotic induction techniques to eliminate tension and negative influences and to strengthen your resolve. Practise them often, make them a healthy habit. They will have a cumulative beneficial effect and will lead to improved mental control and awareness of what you trade.

Looking out in anger

"Never speak loudly to one another unless the house is on fire." (H.W. Thompson)

Of all the negative and self-defeating emotions we allow to afflict us, anger tops the bill as number one killer. Headaches and ulcers are not the worst results of giving it headroom.

Resorting to anger is a habit we develop at a tender age as a conditioned response, as part of our acquired stock of learned avoidance patterns. It flourishes because we fail to recognise it as an abnormal response and because healthier and more effective ways of reacting are seldom seen. We may seek to restrain our outbursts and discover the cause, but anger is cunning in deceit. We are led to seek in the wrong places because the catch is that we are never angry for the reasons we think.

The wrong kind of diet can accentuate the problem by providing a surfeit of energy when there may seem to be no healthy outlet for releasing it. Immaturity, frustration and repressed sexual desires also play their part.

The next few paragraphs call for your active participation.

Play along, otherwise you will read the lyrics and miss the music.

Stress check and make it a thorough one. Read slowly. Now tense and then relax the brow, cheeks, nose, jaw, tongue. Do the same for your neck, shoulders, arms, hands, fingers. Breathe deeply and relax the chest muscles and continue on down. Take your time, this is important. Then stretch and read on.

Search your memory. When did you last experience anger? When did it last flare up into a really noisy row? Go deeply into the memory of it, who was involved, what actually happened to trigger it, how you felt about it at the time. Were you right or wrong? What was it that made you feel upset? Run the whole scenario through in your imagination, make the remembrance as real as you can. Who said what to whom? Be there. Be there now by closing your eyes for two or three minutes. Close your eyes now.

Were you able to relive the experience vividly, to make it real? Good.

How is your pulse rate now, your breathing, the tenseness in your body? Experience it now. Experience the fact that you can create anger in your mind and your body without the presence of another living soul: you do it all to yourself. Nobody is angering you. You always anger yourself.

So what creates the anger, making your emotions run wild and out of control? Search your mind for the reason. Take your time.

Recognise that the cause of anger is only a thought, a belief. A belief can easily be changed. You can learn to see things from a different vantage point in your mind, you can turn the other cheek. With understanding and experience, you can rise above it all and let all anger go.

Stress check now and relax.

Don't waste a precious moment of life in entertaining anger, hate or resentment. Professor Fritz Perls called resentment "the bite that hangs on".

Firstly, recognise that you are free to choose your own reality. You are not here to live up to someone else's expectations. To underline this point, take the well-known case of an elderly spinster who lived in a world of love and romance which she created for herself in her imagination. One night, the story goes, she awakened in horror to find a young, naked man standing at the foot of her bed. "What are you going to do to me?" she asked. "You tell me", he said, "This is your dream".

Fellow pilgrim, this is YOUR life. Choose a golden dream. It can soon become your reality.

The following outline can be adapted to provide a script for a taped recording or for you and a friend to read to one another. Alternatively, induce a light level of hypnosis, opening the eyes at the mental count of three and continuing to read, thoroughly relaxed and centred, reaching beyond the mere words to the spirit of the message.

Get in touch with the anger in your body, all the anger that lies there. Make a fist with either hand and place the anger there; place all the anger you can create inside the fist and hold it, hold it tightly, do it now.

Now inhale a deep breath through the nose, hold, hold, then open the mouth and let out all the air, open your hand and expel all the anger, let it flow out of your body and relax.

Make a second fist, very tightly this time, and in this fist place all the hate you have in your body. Take a deep breath through the nose and hold. Open your mouth and let out all the air, open your hand and expel all the hate, feel it flow out of your body, let it go, relax.

Get in touch with the fear, the jealousy and the envy in your body and cast them out in the same way, holding them tightly and then letting them go.

Deep breathe, count down and relax. Bring in the sunlight, recognised immediately by every cell and by the very essence of your body as the symbol of wisdom, of infinite intelligence.

Forgiveness is an essential step in life, the ever-changing on-flowing cycle of life. Many of us go through every moment of our lives repressing our anger, afraid or ashamed to communicate our innermost thoughts and concerns for fear of losing a friend. Or we suppress our anger, to release it in a flood of uncontrolled emotion, burning up more energy than we expend in a normal working day. Released or suppressed, wherever there is anger there is a forgiveness problem. One person acting sincerely in understanding can release himself and many others from bondage to the dead past.

Into the circle of sunlight bring all those individuals, groups and institutions that will benefit from your forgiveness. To each of them you will see that you are attached by a bond. This bond of negativity is the cause of your anger. Bring in the purple flame now, representing infinite love in action, and see the bonds dissolving as you mentally affirm:

"All that has offended me I forgive, within and without I forgive. Things past, present and future I forgive. I forgive everyone and everything which could possibly require forgiveness. Most of all I forgive myself for first having set everything in motion. All things are cleared up between us all now and forever. All bonds of past judgments and negative interpretations are permanently released. They are free now and I am free too. This I desire and this is so."

Every cell in your body is now polarised to positive energy. You feel vibrant, healthier and happier than you have been for years. You are happy to let go and ignore all the little things that you allowed to trigger your emotions in the past. All you now have to do is breathe deeply, centre and relax. You can trust yourself to stay in charge, to do the best for everyone around you calmly with daily increasing under-standing, very much in charge.

Life you accept as a process of continuous change, an ongoing learning experience. You accept that you can be wrong, that you can fail to satisfy the real or imagined desires of others. Will their reactions matter to you at the same time next year? Ten years from now? Everything will have changed. That's life.

You are no longer the critic and the harsh judge of other people and events. You don't allow other people's faults and weaknesses to distract you from observation of your own.

You know that nobody can be angry with you, they can

only be angry with themselves. Of course they will continue to try to use you to work off their anger and hate, because they want you to hurt, to share the misery which nags them from within. They want to force you to over-react, to waste energy, to weaken you. They seek to dominate and control you, by triggering similar self-destructive emotions of fear and hate and anger in you.

Ignore the static, you know too well where it comes from. Bring the sunlight in, direct love energy to them from the head and the heart. Respond to them with patience and understanding from your centre of calm. Silence is often the best response, while you mentally affirm:

"I am centered in Infinite Being and immune to those who seek to provoke me with negative emotions of fear, hate and anger. Peace and peace and peace to everyone ... this I decree. This is so, now."

Alternatively, until such time as your consciousness is finely tuned, repeat the 'peace and peace' mantra to yourself from the moment the static starts. You will then act with firmness and understanding and not be tricked into responding in kind or reacting in a negative way.

Remember that you do not have to respond immediately or even at all to every event. 'Really' is a suitable response for most occasions. With practice you can make it convey almost anything you want. Californians are delightfully understanding people because they rarely say anything else.

Just pour on the light. It sound ridiculous but it isn't half as silly as rejecting something before you find out if it works for you.

Uncentered, you react to all the minor pressures and stimuli around you, something like a nervous household pet. Centre the mind, withdraw it from the periphery, then the people around you are helped. They will stop looking for the wrongness in you and perhaps be awakened to seek the real reason for their anger.

The only way to win an argument is to avoid it. An argumentative mind is only a flimsy mask for violence and anger. Can a confused mind be open to new ideas? So how do you defuse the anger, so that discussion is possible? By agreeing with the other person. With the person, not the opinion expressed. By saying, for example, 'I agree entirely with what you're saying ... from your personal viewpoint, what you're saying is indisputable.' You leave the door open for your view to be aired: the question of 'rightness' has been eliminated.

If a point you are making is not accepted, don't repeat it. Rephrase it.

And accept criticism graciously, whether it is kindly given or not: 'Thank you. I needed to be reminded of that. Really.'

As the rabbi is reported as saying to the priest: 'Why are we arguing like this? After all, are we not both in the same business? You have a right to express your opinion. I was just expressing God's.'

An interesting variation on the art of turning the other cheek is one of hundreds of incidents recorded by Ananda, Buddha's brother, during forty years of acting as his younger brother's chronicler. Buddha was discussing with some disciples when a stranger walked up to him and spat in his face. His disciples grabbed the man angrily asking 'Lord Buddha, what shall we do with this lunatic? 'Free him', was the response. 'Come here, friend, so that I may thank you. Thanks to you, I now know that there is no anger left in me. How else could I have learned this? Whenever you feel like spitting again, please come and spit on us.'

Health and the young at heart

"Youth is a wonderful thing. What a crime it is to waste it on children." (George Bernard Shaw)

"I didn't arrive at an understanding of the fundamental laws of the Universe by means of the rational mind." (Einstein)

What is living really all about? Why do some people sparkle, never losing the springtime feeling throughout their lives, whilst other people never seem to find it? And why should someone tell you, if the main reason for living is to find out the answers for yourself?

"Lord God forgive all the little tricks I play on you", wrote Robert Frost, "And I'll forgive the big one you played on me."

At the risk of tiresome repetition, we can review some of the evidence to see where it points and perhaps take another step forward on the journey of a thousand miles.

1. Man has the power to direct, focus and control energy in many ways.

2. We can identify one kind of energy as an electro-magnetic flow, source and precise nature presently unclear. Light is a 'living force'. These are two of the forces of nature which all of us can sense. We know that there are others.

3. These apparently intelligent energies permeate, motivate and activate all forms of life, continuously pushing and pulling, attracting and repelling, positive or negative in effect.

4. There is no real beginning or ending, there is a perpetual process of change, apparently accelerating, occasionally following a predictable path or pattern.

5. The cells which form our bodies are constantly changing and being renewed or replaced. They respond to the forces in and around us.

6. Thoughts produce positive or negative electro-magnetic energy which can be directed and measured.

7. We are continuously exposed to the positive and negative influences of individual, family and group thoughts and beliefs.

8. As a species we are scientifically advanced.

9. The average man and many of the most intellectually advanced amongst us have less understanding than an apprentice witch-doctor of the healthy functioning of our bodies, let alone of our minds.

10. We accept opinions and beliefs without testing them for ourselves. When we accept a belief, we don't necessarily live by it, but many are prepared to die for it.

The springtime feeling may have got lost along the way because we fell in love with the objects we created, the toys, finding them easier to relate to and understand than ourselves and other people. We became so fascinated by our powers of deductive reasoning and rational thought that we encouraged this part of our mind to grow. At the same time, we allowed our sixth sense to dwindle and decay, losing nearly all consciousness of the vital two-way link we share with the mutually supportive and sustaining forces of nature.

Quite ordinary men of all times and all ages have discovered how to re-establish this essential natural link. Many of them were uneducated, illiterate men of no fixed abode and no visible means of support. Mohammed, Krishna, Chuang Tzu, Jesus, Mahavir, Gautama Buddha and a host of less publicised 'perfected men' would have been labelled as drop-outs and cult leaders by the media today. They were essentially simple, natural men with simple messages for the ordinary people of their day. Eliminate the fiction and the cant which later chroniclers added to commercialise the teachings and the fundamental message is seen to be the same: 'The Kingdom of God is within you'. Other enlightened men have conveyed the fundamental truth in the following terms:

> The seeds of greatness are found within.
> No one finds God who has not first found himself.

The All is mind, there is no other.
The Way is found in the Inner Sky.
Drop the mind, stop the world.
'Om mani padme hum': God is a ruby in the centre
   of my heart.
The mind that is unknown is the Buddha mind.
The Star that shines in your Eternal Being lights the Way.
When you make the two one, you know God.
Escape from all Masters: the only true Master is within.
Mind is the barrier, no-mind is the Way.
To a mind that is still, the whole world surrenders.

There are many uncharted paths, all leading to the same place. Like flavours of ice-cream, one may appeal to you more than the rest, but be wary of labelling it the best if it is the only one you know.

There are countless other men of fame who learned how to relax and remain active and young at heart well past three score years and ten. Tennyson, Newton, Michaelangelo and Socrates produced some of their best work when they were over eighty. Churchill, who developed the habit of cat-napping throughout his career, was productive to the age of ninety. This habit was shared by Leopold von Ranke, who started writing his 'History of the World' at eighty and completed it at the age of ninety-three. Hundreds of meditative Zen masters live to a ripe old age. One brilliant master, Joshu (Chao Chow Ts'ung Shen), whose inspired teachings survive to this day, started teaching at the age of eighty. He taught for forty years until his death in AD 897.

Catnapping, meditation and hypnotic sleep should not be confused with 'normal' sleep. The normal sleep state is rarely natural in today's stressful world. Sleeping, we remain exposed to the same tensions of daily living but at different levels of consciousness. We can awaken more exhausted physically, mentally and spiritually than when we went to bed. Tranquilisers, alcohol and other chemicals induce the illusion of healthy sleep to the extent that we come to forget what it feels like to benefit from a refreshingly natural night's sleep. The circle closes on itself and deterioration accelerates as the restive mind demands still bigger doses of depressants to counter the negative effects of the earlier doses. By using self-hypnotic techniques, we can overcome the negative influences of tension and consequently direct the natural forces of life to play their assigned role in ensuring our health and survival. To a substantial degree, every man is truly a self-made man.

Use the procedure described in earlier chapters to induce a satisfactory level of relaxation, bringing in the sunlight to accelerate the rejuvenation and healthy renewal of every cell in your body. Follow this with releasing your bonds with the past, releasing all the hurts and resentments, the fears, angers, jealousies and other negative influences which you have directed towards others and which they have directed towards you. Forgive every person, situation and event and most of all, forgive yourself for setting everything in motion. Experience the feeling of the process of 'youthing' reawakening in you the vibrant energies of youth and the spirit of joyous living.

As you practise these mental exercises in a sincere and intelligent way, balancing nightly readings or taped recordings with two or three daily sessions a week, you will become aware of positive subconscious urges, increasing your acceptance of the need for healthy, non-competitive exercise and the elimination from your diet of food and drinks which do not contribute to your general health and wellbeing. Coffee, tea, starchy foods, salt, sugar, and similar products will lose their attraction for you and you will begin to enjoy the more natural flavours and textures of fresh fruit, vegetables, and other wholesome foods. Excessive use of alcohol and other beverages which contain large quantities of sugar will be replaced by making natural water your favourite thirst quencher. If excessive weight is a problem, you will see the wisdom of drinking water both before and after meals and at any time, in the initial stages, when you feel compelled to snack. Water will act as a trigger to strengthen your resolve.

Adapt the following suggestions as your consciousness directs, bringing in the sunlight, in your imagination, and allowing it to radiate to every part of your body:

"*I direct the life-giving energy of light to balance and harmonise all my bodily, mental and spiritual functions, setting the youthing process in operation to rejuvenate and revitalise every aspect and element of the body system in harmony with the one universal life flow.*

"*Every day and in every way I seek to grow in understanding of the healthy functioning of my being and of the natural laws and principles which govern all living things.*

"*I accept all people and events as they are. Anxieties and worries no longer have the power to distract my awareness. I cancel negative influences as they arise with positive understanding, learning more about myself from every single situation and event.*

"*My reverence for life leads me to ever greater understanding and fulfilment. I am a magnet for the vital positive forces of life and for the opportunities for self-expression and development which abound.*

"*I choose my friends wisely and share with them my light, my life, my love, growing younger and more vibrant in health every day. I speak less and listen more, guided by love, kindness and compassion.*

"*I am daily renewed at the bounteous well of light, life and love, for I am a Child of the Universe, with a right and a reason for being here.*

"*I choose to live in health and harmony with the progressive movement and evolution of mankind, at peace with God and with all mankind.*

"*All this I affirm, I desire it and it is so. It is so.*"

Repeating earlier observations, it is important to accept until such time as you have experienced it for yourself, that the speed and degree of success of the affirmation procedure is influenced by several factors. It is irrelevant how the effectiveness of the procedure is judged by the conscious mind: in these matters, the conscious mind is an ass. If the messages are conveyed to the subconscious levels in the relaxed, hypnotic state, this is all that is necessary. In this relaxed state, the enhanced ability to visualise and feel the positive force of imagination on the physical plane is certain to produce the desired results and your mind will rapidly adjust itself to a perfect working relationship. This point will be amplified later when the use of professional cassette tapes is discussed.

Zen, with its customary simplicity of expression and economy of words, offers a joyful affirmation for greeting each new day: 'How sweet the dawn, how great to look around and know that I am still six feet over ground.'

You may find that you were comfortable with some of the friends you chose in the past because of the complementary weaknesses you shared. Now their appeal will diminish as you see the negative consequences of the relationship. Let them go. Your example rather than your opinion will be the best help you can give them and you know why: nobody ever learns anything worthwhile by being told. First you must want to find out. Nor will you ever be friendless; the right kind of relationships will establish themselves simply because, in Nature, like attracts like.

As your self-understanding increases, people young and old will be drawn to you to seek your help and advice. Direct the light of the sun and your love to them mentally, caring but never accepting their problems into your own consciousness, shielding yourself always against negative emanations. Centre and let Infinite Intelligence show you how to help them to become self-reliant and to accept their responsibility for their own lives and actions. You may find people who will seek a solution to the problems that their ways of thinking and living have caused, but who will not accept any solution which involves changing their negative attitudes or lifestyle. Help them with time or money and they will waste it in the same way that they are wasting their own. The right responses will arise out of the depths of your compassion, from the calm centre of dignity that is developing in you.

Those irritating or worrying things which you allowed to

upset you in the past can now be seen as opportunities for rising above them. The more you find yourself opening to this positive way of responding the more fun and fulfilment you will find in this intriguing game of life.

Bodywork

At the same time as your subconscious intelligence is reviewing and renewing all functions of your body, transmuting light and other subtle forces, providing heat and energy in response to changes in the environment, it has other simultaneous duties to perform, unceasingly, day and night. A perpetual cockpit check is in progress, more or less in the following form:

Oxygen, carbon dioxide levels checked, lung functions OK.

Joints, skeletal framework, muscles serviced, relaxed, set to instant response.

Blood pressure normal, breathing free, adjustable.

Immune system balanced, hormonal levels checked.

Nerve tissue responses normal.

Cholesterol, chemical responses of all systems, brain, glands, emotional and other responses, all normal.

Vision, hearing, taste, smell, touch senses and instinct switched to full alert. Thyroid gland balanced.

Metabolism setting correct. Limbs co-ordinated.

Heartbeat, blood vessels, arteries, capilliaries all functioning properly, no blockages or deposits formed.

Blood count correct, blood chemistry, salts, sugar, calcium mixture correct, pressure rechecked.

Digestive and elimination systems balanced, functioning OK.

Production of digestive enzymes and insulin, regulation of blood sugar operating correctly: pancreas OK.

Production of bile, proteins, fats, carbohydrates and enzymes, all levels balanced. Liver OK.

Blood clotting mechanism, spleen operational.

Adrenal glands checked, OK. Kidney filter functional, extraction of surplus salts and water from blood supply operational, waste transport to bladder free, no blockages. Exit valve controls OK.

Pelvic and sex organs on standby OK.

Spinal column responding to all signals, fully flexible, all interconnections sound.

Shock absorption and emergency services, on alert.

All sections activated, fully responsive and functional.

Simultaneous operational check on all circuits continues, switching on to sleep mode ....

.... and as a home is more than the sum total of its individual parts, so is the body. Body, mind and spirit are only separate in words and thought. The same intelligent energy is inherent in every atom and cell, responsive to signals from subconscious control and acting in harmony with physical, mental, spiritual and other influences, both 'inside' and 'outside' the system.

Block your ears with the tips of your index fingers and listen to the anatomy at work. Take a few minutes to tune in and identify some of the distinctive deeper rhythms.

Fortunately, at the conscious levels, there is no need to concern ourselves with the intricate functioning of the body mechanisms. Nothing more is required than to keep alert and avoid confusing the driver. Even though it is only a rented vehicle, take good care of it and it will take you wherever you choose to go.

Success

"All paths differ but the way is always the same".

(Camac II)

- **That certain feeling**

How do you personally define success, what is success to you? If you feel vague or unclear at the conscious level, you give your subconscious nothing to work with. As a preliminary step, take a moment to write down your personal definition of success. Suspend any interest in reading what follows until you can express your feelings about it in less than twenty words. Later, you may choose to modify or expand it as the basis for an affirmative post-hypnotic statement.

A written expression of what you truly feel about success is vital to the purpose of this chapter, which is to show you how to attain it.

Resistance to instructions of the kind given in the opening paragraph is derived from frustrations, imaginary or real, which you experienced during childhood. Once this is seen to be true, the limiting habit can be dropped.

- **Imagination, friend or foe**
  Stress check and relax.
Better still, sit for five minutes and do nothing.

To the degree that you can do this, your success, in every sense of the word, is assured. Get accustomed to inducing the relaxed, blissful state. This way, you transcend the intellectual mind, you drop the monkey. You then have a choice. You can clear and reprogramme your own mind or allow the world to continue to programme it for you. Because the biggest secret of success is simply to become your own best friend.

- **Fear of success**
  You can use your favourite hypnotic relaxation technique to determine the extent to which you have acquired a subconscious fear of success by examining some of your impressions.

For example, who or what is responsible for your present status in life? Perhaps your working days started by having to accept the first job that was offered, because of heavy unemployment in your home area or other limitations. You just lacked the initiative to seek further afield. Then you perhaps found that you were in a comfortable rut, that idiot's grave with exits at both ends. Who needs success anyway? Nobody likes successful people; they have very few friends. At least as a failure you are in the majority, you have lots of friends to commiserate with you, to console you, to confirm that it wasn't really your fault. People will recognise you as a good loser, you can be proud of that. Life after all, is just a silly game, with rules you don't understand so why take anything seriously?

To what extent have you accepted that you need capital to start, you need a degree to get anywhere, that the whole system is against you from the beginning? What other negative illusions have you accepted as truths?

When you are looking from the wrong place through a fog of confusion and negativity, you trip over opportunities that you fail to see until later, when the bruises appear. You know now that your subconscious or superconscious mind only responds to your dominant thoughts and feelings. When you telegraph anxiety, fear and confusion you forfeit all hope of focusing your mindpower on achieving your real desires.

- **Friends and other diversions**
  There is no virtue in failure. Its effects are often disguised with the false faces of martyrdom, resignation and tired good humour. The truth is that frustration and failure breed cruel, bitter and resentful people who can infect the unwary with the lifetime loser's germ.

So choose your friends with care. Avoid those who enjoy gossiping and criticising everyone and everything around them. They are seeking distraction from their own feelings of worthlessness. Send them light from your heart and keep your own counsel. They can never be helped directly with words, no matter how carefully you choose them. Words can only serve to point them to a place beyond their illusions and superstitions but the fear that led them to create the twilight world they inhabit will continue to hold them there. What they fail to learn from words they may come to learn from your example.

In brief: play the game of life on your terms and on your values and share it with people who enrich your experience.

Success or failure is our individual responsibility. Once you accept the fact that failure is primarily due to your own ignorance, you are well on the way to success. Other people may have played a secondary role in contributing to your failure. Forgive them and feel compassion for them for they are at least one step further back from understanding than you are today. See what this means? You have a clear advantage over other people already!

So forgive yourself for earlier misunderstandings and for ever doubting your own self-worth.

Relax, visualise that purifying purple flame and affirm:

'All negative thoughts, ideas, influences and self-limiting beliefs which I have accepted in the past will be transmuted to strong, positive influences for success in every phase of my life, on the count of three... one ... two ... three.'

Express thanks and release the flame.

● **Developing imagination**

A full appreciation of the effectiveness of self-hypnotic techniques may be beyond the power of your imagination, but this will not be for long, because it is in the very exercise of the imagination that the greatest power available to mankind becomes apparent.

Major advances in the course of human development are never initiated by organisations, whether political, industrial or religious. They are inevitably born in the imagination of a single individual. They are always the product of one original mind.

The subconscious mind, the source of your creative imagination, is both reactive and reflexive. This has long been identified as the law of correspondence, one of the vital principles of life first recognised by Hermes Trismegistus. Basically, how it works is that whatever you seed in the subconscious mind grows, blossoms and multiplies. What you sow there you most surely reap. Contemplate right action or visualise a desired result with feeling, and the subconscious immediately sets the appropriate response in motion ... and keeps on responding until you change the message. It therefore works for you or against you, depending strictly on how you focus it. Relax, for example, and dwell on a clear idea of success, let it expand in you, allowing your feelings, your emotions, to fall in line with your desires. Feel the thrill of it. Affirm it. From then on, your subconscious mindpower will use you as a channel to bring your desires to reality. You don't have to think about what to do. If action is required, the infinite intelligence of the subconscious mind will direct and control your course of action at a level which the conscious mind recognises and must obey.

Be absolutely clear that no mental effort is required on your part. Attempt to apply pressure on the subconscious mind and you imply that there is opposition to your wishes and opposition is exactly what you will get. When you have gained some confidence in yourself as a result of your experiences with the introductory exercises, you will find it easy to approach your daily relaxation sessions with pleasure and anticipation. Force yourself in any way and you obviously defeat the whole purpose of the exercise, which is to relax.

- **Management of time**

   Yet another monkey mind dilemma is that the more problems you create for yourself, the less time you seem to have to relax. The fact is that you always have time, you just have to learn how to manage it. You could skip a few hours of televison viewing and try to relax and do nothing, but you would find yourself worrying about what you might be missing. After all, you indulge yourself in television viewing because you need to relax, right? How much of it actually bores and irritates you? How much of it enriches and inspires you? There are people who actually watch late night horror movies for relaxation and entertainment! Take ten and ponder what you have learned from television viewing in the last month that has added to your understanding and self-confidence. Then decide to be more selective and find healthier ways of using your leisure time.

- **The creative mode**

   So the two great secrets of success are both simple ones: be your own best friend and do nothing. That's right, do nothing. Loll about, relax, free from any rogue feelings of guilt that you may be wasting valuable time being unbusy, unproductive. Skip out from the world of senseless chatter and trivial pastimes. Hang loose, lazy, let go all life-denying thoughts and activities so that you leave space for your real needs and true desires to surface. How your needs and desires will be met is not your concern, just visualise a clear model of how you want things to be. Sustain this awareness at other times and soon, and very soon indeed, it will require no conscious thought on your part. It will become a positive conditioned reflex and the subconscious powerhouse will be firmly in charge.

- **Affirming your success**
  Are you happy with your earlier definition of success? Success is something which you have to prepare yourself for in every way, in body, mind and spirit. Success is one of the vital laws of nature. It is an essential positive lifeforce, forever seeking new forms of expression at the level we experience as reality.

  Feeding your subconscious with a vague, confused picture of what you mean by success is like leaving the clues out of a crossword puzzle. The subconscious doesn't play guessing games. If it's confused, it does nothing. So spell out what you want and tolerate no limitations.

  Here is a short form of affirmation which you can use effectively when you feel like it:

  "Daily I move from success to success as I grow in understanding of my true purpose in life and moment to moment I see it unfold."

  When you feel like it, it works for you.

- **Success in your job**
  If you are presently employed, you may find that you can relate your circumstances to this example.

  You have spent some time in your present employment. At first the job seemed interesting, even exciting, and your boss seemed to be a reasonable fellow. Now you have the feeling that your efforts are not fully appreciated and that you are not being paid what you're worth.

  Is that how it is with you today? If so, you have just succeeded in blowing it again! You have activated the instant eject button, with your own head. See how it works?

You have told the subconscious that you see opposition to your needs in your present job, and the subconscious immediately sets about severing your connection with it. Without, may we add, receiving any indication that you need another job. The process is entirely automatic, the situation is now entirely out of your conscious control. No warning bells are ringing because your subconscious expects you to know how your own mind functions.

And when your job folds, as it assuredly will one way or another, your puzzled boss will say "I honestly don't know what got into him. His whole attitude changed overnight. He was one of our best men. I had great plans for him."

Shattering, isn't it? You can never be fired by anyone except yourself. All phases of your life are exclusively under your own control. There are no exceptions.

What is 'right action' in this case? Let's say someone or something gives you the impression that you are not being paid what you're worth. Immediately reject this as a negative attitude. Relax fully and release any and all of the negativity that has accumulated in the cells of your body and in the consciousness that motivates them.

Use a relaxation technique to review your situation. Return to the day you were hired for the job. Recall your attitude of alertness, interest and concentration at the job interview. You did everything you could to get the job and you got it. Have you since done everything you could to keep it? Is this the same excited, interested, dynamic you? What old habits have contributed to you giving less than one-hundred-percent to the job in hand? What have you done to fine-tune your skills and expand your job knowledge? Have you a clear concept of what your job calls for in know-how, problem solving and accountability and do you know how these functions translate into cash value? Do you know how your performance is rated? Have you learned how to sustain peak performance? Are you satisfied with less? Have you learned how to discuss job progress with your boss?

You may not yet know what to do for the best but you can surely see what not to do. Realise that how you feel most of the time is the image that you present to the people around you. Dogs and small children, for example, are never fooled by mere words and postures, and wives and bosses are not fooled for long. You mirror your deepest feelings in your attitude, and it is on this attitude that you are judged. Decide to expand your knowledge of personal relationships and widen your vision by seeking experience in Blake's managerial grid, job evaluation, psychometric interviewing techniques and other experiential subjects. You can live without these, but why learn the hard way tomorrow what you can learn the easy way today?

Learn to relax and let your consciousness tell you what you need in order to do the job better, how to work smarter rather than longer and harder, how to increase the money value of the service you provide. When your consciousness awakens fully to the dulling influence of repetitive, destructive thinking and negative attitudes, it provides space for intuitive imaginings and more: you realise that creative ideas and opportunities are all around you. They have never ceased to clamour for your attention. You can foresee new product trends and anticipate market demand because you have always had the power of precognition, you just didn't let it develop. Visualise the ideal in your job or business. Compare it with the present day situation. Why the shortfall? A year from now there will be new opportunities and improved ways of doing things. New needs will be apparent which have not yet been expressed. What are these opportunities, ways and needs now, right now?

For a while, the monkey mind will continue to behave like some clown waving in the background during a televised interview and repetitive nonsense will intrude. The moment you become aware of this, feed it the alphabet to repeat backwards. It will soon get the message and stay in its place. Take particular care to use your words and thoughts constructively at all times.

You will find that you can apply the same patient skills

to problem solving. A problem develops because it attracts more error as it grows, obscuring the original cause. The solution is born at the same time as the problem as part of the seed, in much the same way that every living cell carries the seed of its own dissolution. Ignore what the problem has become and trace back to its origin. The one and only correct solution will then be clearly visible.

- **Success in game-playing**

Play games to relax and have fun, unless you aim to become a professional. By all means develop and improve your game-playing skills, but direct your ego drive and competitive energies into your work, not into golf, tennis or squash. This way you will ensure a four-way benefit for yourself, your game, your business and your friends and associates.

Play to play. Playing to win is like painting by numbers or dancing to reach a particular spot on the floor. Play up and play the game.

- **The way ahead**

Everything in life has a latent capacity for perpetual change and development and you and your job are no exceptions. From time to time, take the time to review your present and future aspirations. Switch your mind to the creative mode, let your imagination flow and expand, free from all concern for time and other social limitations.

Here is a general purpose form of affirmation which you can modify and improve to suit whatever purpose your awakening consciousness suggests:

"The job I have chosen has chosen me and I am here to master it.

I claim my birthright to choose my own destiny and I choose success in all things.

The infinite intelligence of my creative mind draws on my inborn talents and inspires me to excel in every way, contributing fully to the needs and aspirations of those I serve and those who serve me.

I attract opportunities for progress. My creative energies and actions are stimulated and directed to play their part in

*the perpetual development and evolution of all mankind.
This is my desire and this is so."*

It is up to you to decide when you are prepared to be more
specific and to list exactly what you desire, briefly and to
the point. Establish priorities by date order, to help you fix
them clearly in your mind. Take the time to prepare a list
carefully in the form of an affirmation and refer to it constantly until it becomes part of your consciousness. The full
procedure is as follows:

- Stress check and relax, letting your consciousness expand,
  free from all negativity.

- List your aims and desires.

- Acknowledge your inalienable right to achieve them.

- Confirm that they will be met and specify dates.

- Affirm your understanding.

- Visualise the successful outcome.

The following is suggested as a suitable form of affirmation
as far as income is concerned:

*'As and from (date) I shall merit and receive an income
of (amount) monthly, increasing by (percent) annually.*

*I claim this as part of my birthright, recognising any sense
of limitation as false.*

*I call on the infinite intelligence of my creative mind to
guide me in achieving this income and to direct me in its
proper use.*

I desire this and it is so.'

- **Born free**

    Only a man who allows his imagination to develop is
ever truly free.

    It is your birthright and also your responsibility to allow
your spirit to experience all the wonders of human existence,
to develop your latent talents to the full, to flourish, to radiate
success, not merely to shine.

    Not surprisingly, the immortal bard captured a similar
theme when he wrote "This above all – to thine own self be
true; and it must follow, as the night the day, thou canst not

then be false to any man."

When you draw on a different level of understanding your whole outlook on life naturally changes but this is only half the story. The source of understanding itself, the subconscious or superconscious mind, expands and draws on the limitless power within it. Its latent capacity for infinite development awakens. It is for this reason that no matter how much your consciousness expands you will always be able to say "there is more to me than this."

Wealth

"If you can actually count your money then you are not a wealthy man." (Paul Getty)

This is a practical guide to wealth, so you will benefit to the extent that you allow yourself to become involved. You will require paper and pencil now to respond to two personal questions and to complete a five minute exercise. If this is presently inconvenient, skip the chapter until you can comply.

The exercise is necessary because we are using words to communicate at the conscious level, consequently you can best benefit by making a 'before and after' comparison of your feelings.

The question to which a written response is required is: what is your greatest asset and how much is it worth?

The exercise requires you to write down the words 'I am wealthy', adding whatever thought the phrase triggers in your subconscious, whatever thought comes to mind. Repeat this procedure as many times as you wish, each time spelling out the phrase 'I am wealthy' and then adding whatever new thought is triggered by the statement.

You should find it possible to produce six to ten different responses and this is adequate for our purpose.

Kindly reread the instructions and complete the five minute exercise now.

Keep your response handy to refer to later.

Most of us have been encouraged to believe that the more we apply ourselves to developing the intellect, the greater the possibility of achieving wealth and success. Our educational systems are largely dedicated to this end. This, from a Zen viewpoint, is like harnessing a horse to the back of a wagon in the forlorn hope that it will somehow free itself, climb over the wagon and play an active role between the shafts. Because the intellect arose from the consciousness of man. From the original conceptual error of individuality and separateness the 'I' concept, the ego, was born. All our subsequent thoughts have contributed to the illusion that the intellect is superior to the consciousness from which it arose. Self-hypnosis and meditation are techniques which lead to a reawakening of our awareness to the true nature of the 'I', to a return to consciousness. The problems and limitations which the intellectual mind creates can then be seen for what they are. The original error can be corrected, the false start forgotten and a fresh beginning can be made.

This is not to deny that the intellectual mind is a useful tool when it is properly used and its limitations are properly understood. However, it is from our consciousness that we derive the unique powers of visualisation and imagination. We can create images. Look around you. Is there any manmade object that was not first imaged? What we may require is a clearer understanding of the nature of creative imagination so that we can call it into play at will, whenever we choose to use it.

Imagination, in the broadest sense, is our personal link with everything we choose to regard as Divine, just as breathing is a link with our environment. Another way of regarding it is that it is our personal connection between the formed Universe and the formless energy from which all things manifest. As an exercise in imagination, we can speculate that all natural elements in the Universe and beyond have been created at a greater imaginative level: they have first been imaged. This is not an original concept. You may recall the Biblical comment 'In his own image, God created man.' 'Man was imaged' is possibly a more correct translation from the original text. Anyone who has ever translated from one language to another will know the problem. The level of understanding and the bias of the translator cannot fail to influence the final text.

It is this connector, this power of the imagination, which self-hypnosis and meditation awaken to alert the mind to the accumulation of negativity and bias which we have unwittingly absorbed. The first step is therefore to become aware of the extent to which we are handicapped by what we have absorbed in the past.

How comfortable do you feel about the concept of wealth? Wish yourself, 'wealth, health and happiness'. Comfortable? Given a choice, which would you choose above all others? Happiness? Probably health, right? Here's the good news. You don't have to choose. You don't have to limit yourself in any way. Wealth, health and happiness are only a sprinkling of the gifts of a bountiful Nature which recognises and accepts no limitations. None. The concept of limitation exists only to the extent that it is created in your own head, in your own imagination. Think it, believe it, feel it, it becomes your own reality, a negative reality.

Your past conditioning made you think it. Where wealth is concerned, you certainly don't want to be greedy and perhaps do someone else out of his share, right? His share of what? Unlimited resources? Life offers an abundance, an overflowing: there is more than enough of everything for everyone. What then, the doubting mind will ask, of famine and pestilence, to name but a few? Stay with the simpler personal level first. When you have thoroughly explored and understood this level, understanding of the influence of ignorance on a grand scale will suddenly dawn on you. To resolve any problem, irrespective of complexity and scale, seek first to understand how the problem was born. Seek back to the original error, to the original lack of consciousness.

What other negatives have been absorbed? Do you agree, for example, that it is better to be poor and healthy than rich and sick? Poverty is a negative state of mind, a result of mental confusion. Why create limitations? Choose to be wealthy and healthy.

Then you will have heard expressions like 'filthy lucre' and 'money is the root of all evil'. Money in itself is not good or bad, any more than any form of power is good or bad. How it is used can help or hurt, depending on the intention of the person who controls it. Lack of money is nearer the root of all evil. Financial abundance is part of everyone's birthright. Nature holds back nothing.

When you truly appreciate what life has to offer, you will never limit yourself to amassing a large fortune. Nor is there ever a need to join the high-flying low-life and become wealthy by exploiting the weaknesses of others. Feel compassion for those who do, for they expose themselves to a terrible correction. Everything they gain in wealth they lose in peace of mind.

And to answer two earlier questions, the imaginative power of your subconscious mind is your greatest asset and it is of inestimable value, when you learn how to use it correctly. It responds to what you feel is true, not to what you say, think, know or believe. Your heart must be involved as well as your head. Eliminate negativity and your feelings can then be brought effortlessly under direct conscious control.

Kindly revert to the exercise you were asked to complete and examine it for negative attitudes, self-limitations and evasions.

When you saw the chapter heading, you knew what the word 'wealth' implied. 'I am wealthy in my friends', for example, is an evasive response, a shying away from a natural desire for material wealth, a denial of a part of human life. 'I am wealthy, but others are wealthier.' Do you have what you can handle? If not, why not? 'I am wealthy in everything except health.' Really. So if you made your wealth, how did you unmake your health? If you don't know, what is stopping you from finding out? And so on .....

Change each sentence to a positive affirmation, and use this as part of your positive reconditioning until such time as all the subtle forms of negativity are revealed and transmuted to positive influences.

Eliminate all limiting thoughts because you know that you have every right to wealth, no less than any man who has ever lived. This is part of your birthright, waiting to be claimed. Know that your awakening consciousness will guide and direct you to wealth and to the proper use of it. And accept no limitations, for wealth is only one of the many forms of living energy which we are empowered to direct. Direct it lifewards and the flow will increase.

When you say 'good health' you know what you mean, you can feel it. When you say 'good wealth', say it and feel it in exactly the same way.

At least once a day, visualise the inflow and outflow of wealth through your bank account, increasing, accumulating. Be wealth, sing it, dance it. Feel the thrill of financial abundance. Make a list of your most imaginative plans for development and expansion and visualise them all in their completed form. Live with the pictures in your mind and know that the means of achievement are the province of the infinite intelligence of your subconscious mind.

The following is a general form of affirmation:

"The living energy of wealth is mine to attract, to direct and enjoy as part of the fullness of life. Every day I grow in understanding of its power and I am guided and directed to use it well.
This I desire and this is so."

The flow of wealth is the very bloodstream of the world's economy and, as such, it is a vital part of Man's evolution. Use the lifeline to your subconscious to ensure you play your rightful part in it. No one has more right than you.

Love Marriage and Model Mates

"Two's company, three's a crowd. Right now, there's you, me and your ego". (Camac II)

The danger in accumulating knowledge is that it not only overloads the attic of the mind, it blocks the view from the windows. It pays to check the accumulation from time to time and clear out the junk. For this, all you require right now is paper, pen and privacy. If you find it inconvenient to devote fifteen minutes or so to the exercise which follows, skip the entire chapter until later date. It can wait. Reading on may further increase your knowledge, but it will do nothing for your understanding.

All set and ready to write? Write out the following sentence:

I am a good husband (or wife or lover, whichever is appropriate to your present status), and then add whatever thought comes to mind.

Stress check, relax and again write 'I am a good .... husband/wife/lover .... and allow your mind to react and complete the statement.

Do this at least half a dozen times, writing the full statement each time, adding your thoughts and the two words: 'Thank you'.

Kindly reread the instruction and complete the exercise now to your own satisfaction.

Did it feel rather strange writing out the words 'Thank you' to yourself? Curious that, we don't think it strange to talk to ourselves subvocally whenever we are alone.

File your notes away safely until later. As a woman, the privacy of your handbag is suggested. As a man, take good care to avoid the experience of hearing an outburst of hysterical laughter indicating that your wife has chanced on your hiding place.

The generally accepted social convention of marriage can prove a difficult one to live with, because it is not necessarily what Nature intended for men and women. Like democracy, it has evolved as a means of satisfying most of the needs of a majority. When the rules and limitations are thoroughly understood, frustrations can be avoided and the role-playing can be enjoyed as a pleasant form of educational experience. For many people, living together can become a comfortable way of maturing as men and women. As males and females, we respond mainly to our inborn animal urges which, though essential to the continuance of the species, can result in considerable imbalance if allowed to dominate our relationships.

Stress check, relax and see how your mind responds to the following questions. You will not find a list of answers in the book. The questions are intended to give you a feeling for where you are looking from and to indicate to you how much, or how little, you can see from there. Snap answers will indicate that it is your intellect which is responding at the customary superficial level. Relax and go deeper.

What is a woman's basic need in life? Is a man's the same?

Is the 'father' concept a natural one, or are all men better cast to act the role of tribal guardians and uncles?

What transcends or is beyond intellect, logic, emotions, sentimentality?

Are your thoughts reality? Are they yours?

We see the wrong in others. Why?

Can you transform another person?

Does understanding require effort?

Do we seek to learn or only to fit things into the framework of what we think we know?

How do you distinguish between revelation and self-delusion?

What doors can open to a mind which is egotistical, cynical, insensitive, argumentative or doubting?

Have you ever inspired anybody? Why not?

Do we express opinions because we know or because we don't?

What you planned to say, what you said, what you

should have said — why do they differ?

If you were not intended to take responsibility for your own destiny, why were you given consciousness?

A lifelong partnership can be a sorry affair if the partners have not matured to the extent of understanding themselves. The most common situation is to find that one dominant partner, probably the less capable one, enforces his will on the other, seemingly denying the other a choice. In this way the marriage partnership, which should be a sharing experience, becomes a one-sided affair. One partner indulges in selfish pursuits while the other suffers, sometimes in silence, accepting the twilight-life of a secondary role. In this case, one plus one make less than two, and both are at fault in allowing the life-denying situation to persist.

Teasing is a childish habit which some thoughtless partners never outgrow. They find a malicious joy in causing irritation and discomfort to others. They get a negative boost by draining their victims' energy. An unwary person can allow the irritation to become a pain in the neck, or elsewhere. The constant teaser is unwittingly doing what a constant drip can do to a stone. Help them with understanding: light can still reach to minds that are lost in the shadows.

When one marital partner matures faster than the other, the favoured one may be tempted to leave the laggard to his own devices. After all, with maturity you learn to be independent, finding pleasure in your own company. But the reverse is also the case: misery needs the company of others as a means of seeking distraction from itself. The laggard needs your patient understanding more than ever as he will feel compelled to seek diversions and justification for his form of existence elsewhere. Bars, clubs, and churches can be filled with immature people, all seeking vainly to find there something which can only be found in themselves.

Unlike the male, whose role in the reproduction of the species is a trivial one, the female has a prolonged part to play for which Nature prepares her from birth. For this reason alone, most females mature early and have less illusions about the fundamental principles of life than males. Unfortunately

"Why Father – now we even dream the same dreams!!"

the unnatural religious and social conventions which govern behaviour in many lands encourage the male to adopt the dominant role, so that the female is forced to use guile to attract and retain the male's interest and support for herself and her children. This necessity to inflate the male ego further aggravates the problem, lessening the chances that the male will ever awaken to his natural role, and further decreasing the possibility of either of them enjoying an interdependent, fulfilling life. Against this unnatural background, we rear our children and later wonder why they seek every means of breaking with established traditions, as they vainly search for a more rewarding, non-neurotic form of society. This, against a backdrop of a culture which is hellbent on producing machines with smart brains to replace people who have never learned to develop their own.

Most of us have at least a conscious desire for peace and harmony in our lives, but the attainment of our desires is outside the scope of the conscious mind. We need to discover what concepts our subconscious mind has accepted, because these are what influence our destiny.

A female finds purpose in life in loving and being loved. She attains maturity and fulfilment as a woman when her first child is born.

No love on Earth is as deep and strong as a mother's love for her child, and there is no greater loyalty than that which she offers the man she can trust.

A male's primary drive is in proving his manhood. He matures when he understands his purpose in life and he finds fulfilment in attaining it.

When a male proves his manhood to himself, he has no need to prove it to anyone else. Until such time as he does, he can seek in countless futile ways to prove it to others. The ways he chooses can include all kinds of unnecessary risk-taking, from fast driving, mountain climbing, sky-diving and other strenuous sports to sexual excesses, competitive drinking and other equally mindless activities. When the primary reason for risktaking is an obsession or compulsion — a conscious or subconscious urge — to put life at risk, to dice with death, there is a lesson to be learned. For there is nothing in life we have to prove to ourselves or anyone else. We have all been found worthy of the gift of life. What prize or proof is greater than this? The motivation is fear, fear that he is less than a man. He will try to escape from himself by seeking the approval and comfort of others with whom he shares the common bond of mental confusion.

Throughout Man's history, ambitious men have found it easy to exploit this misdirected male search for manhood, never finding it difficult to recruit the gullible and the imma-ture to 'prove themselves' in battle and be 'decorated' for acts of gross stupidity. Yet, as in all things, there is a positive aspect, the yang to the aggressive yin. The defending males are provided with the opportunity to attain early manhood, because the defence of life — of self and friends and family — is a healthy, natural instinct in every man. In this way, out of one man's weakness comes forth strength.

None of this is new to you, but it may have been forgotten. So where do you go from here? Understanding is never enough unless you live by it. If only for the sake of amuse-ment, accept the possibility that you are primarily responsible for everything that is unpleasant in your life, that you are unconsciously allowing yourself to be trapped in habits which trigger negative responses in your partner. You can distract yourself by playing the judge, deciding what is right or wrong, fair or unfair, but that gets you nowhere. We may never be objective enough. Instead, select one recurrent problem to start with and see what happens when you change the part you play in it. For example, anticipate a recurrent need in-stead of waiting to be reminded of it when you are involved in doing something else. When you see the results you will be encouraged to apply your increased awareness to the more subtle forms of friction in your life.

The following is a useful affirmation for marital partners:

"There are no secrets. I release all of the past. I forgive everyone, including myself for failing to see the leading role I have played in all the events of my life. I can never be hurt or shocked or saddened by myself or anyone else unless I

choose to be. With awareness, I rise above these things.

"I am at peace with everyone, including myself. I have the health, strength and understanding to live every moment of my life to the full.

"Life is peace and light and love and harmony and I am a living expression of it.

"This I decree. This is so".

You may now wish to compare the feelings you recorded in the earlier exercise with a selection of those expressed on the subject of maturity and marriage by couples attending hypnotic training courses.

Wives: My husband understands my womanly need to feel secure in his love. He demonstrates his understanding in a thousand gentle ways. He respects me, both as a woman, and as the mother of our children.

Husbands: The joy my wife expresses in our home and family, I deeply share. I delight in seeing her develop and use her intuition and other inborn talents. She enriches our living experience in every way. Her love is my inspiration.

Both: Neither of us manipulates or dominates the other, our life is an adventure we share. We share the same preferences for people, places and things and we understand why.

We never treat the other as second best, in public or in private. We are interdependent, each competent to act alone or together as one. There is nothing we cannot freely discuss and amicably resolve. Why take the other for granted when you can ask: 'Is this what you wish too'?

Our marriage is emotionally sound and we choose to keep it that way.

We both find harmony in the sexual expression of our love.

Our children 'are not cups to be filled, but lamps to be lit'. We share the joy of seeing them develop in an atmosphere of love and understanding. We enjoy a sense of freedom in our hearts and in our home.

Our shared life is in our own hands as surely as our own. We chose one another as companions for life. We have never made a better choice.

We blossom in each other's company — we can even surprise ourselves.

The above observations were, in fact, post-hypnotic responses to the question: 'What is an ideal partner and an
ideal marital relationship?' To the extent that the experience
you have chosen differs from these ideals, you may find it
rewarding to ask yourself why.

As a man, when did you last hold your wife's hand, not
out of habit or custom or as a young lover, but out of compassion for a fellow pilgrim who held your hand many times
in your journey from confusion to consciousness? You owe
her no less for sharing her life with you. Hers was the voice
that cried out as you wandered in the wilderness of your
mind: reach out and take her hand. The true pattern of
evolution can only unfold when two minds, forever young,
learn to merge as one. Then, and only then, the blossom-
ing ......

If you and your life's companion can add to the list of
observations it would be a joy to meet you, if only to know
why you are reading this book.

Prayer, meditation and hypnosis II

"O Lord, Thou knowest how busy I must be this day: if I forget Thee, do not Thou forget me." (Sir Jacob Ashley, 1579-1652)

Religion serves a purpose when it is not used as a comforter or a drug to the mind or as a means of manipulating the gullible by exploiting their fears, guilts and superstitions — 'fleecing sheep', as Gurdjieff termed it. Those religions which claim exclusive salvationary rights for their particular flock contribute substantially to the instability in the world by dividing man from man. The human dilemma has always been that the more man allows his imagination to be fired by one of the hundreds of religious concepts of divinity, the further he becomes removed from understanding and respect for life and humanity.

Prayer can work wonders for the few still blessed with childlike innocence and faith, those 'born of a virgin mind'. We can draw a simple parallel with electricity. You only need to know how to switch on the light, you don't need to know how the circuit works. But if all you know is how to operate the switch and now the circuit is fused, you could lose all your faith in switches. The prayer circuit fuses when you lean too often on the switch.

The way prayer doesn't work is to plead for help with all your emotional eloquence and will-power, coupled with lavish promises of uncharacteristically good behaviour in the future. The immutable law of reversed effect comes smartly into play. Unwittingly, you are telegraphing to your subconscious intelligence that you sense opposition to your request. Fear or worry being your dominant emotion, the subconscious acts on this and immediately sets about dealing with an obstacle that doesn't exist. 'Repel boarders' is the order which takes precedence over all others whenever your survival appears to be threatened from without. All hands will stay on full-time defensive alert until the erroneous order is cancelled.

The innocent and the faithful automatically do the right

thing. There is no room for doubt or concern in their minds when they pray for help to the Power they trust. Their belief is absolute, they know that they have only to articulate their need for it to be met. If they seek health and prosperity and their motives are pure, in harmony with the natural laws of being, then their needs will be met. Their innocent faith will be further strengthened. The only requirements have been met. The conscious mind has relaxed and passed a blueprint to the subconscious, a clear picture of the successful realisation of the desire. All levels of mind are at peace and in harmony, all tuned to the same waveband, seeing the event as a reality. Infinite Intelligence immediately sets about making it manifest, bringing it into being at the mortal plane of reality. An infinite variety of possible options or probabilities are always waiting patiently in the wings, eager and willing to be called to centre stage.

Repentance and seeking forgiveness through petition and prayer fool nobody except ourselves, unless they brings forth an immediate and permanent change in the way we feel, live and act. Self-torture, by dwelling on feelings of remorse and guilt, only contributes more to the illusion that forgiveness is won by suffering. We can only be found guilty of self-ignorance, for failing to see the ridiculous limitations we put on ourselves. For failing to see the jest.

Zen meditation has something in common with the self-hypnosis state and each contributes to a deeper understanding of the other. Zen is a way of living, not a religious doctrine. Spiritual materialism, with its concepts of divinity and a life hereafter, is seen as being as relevant to understanding our true nature as all the other illusions we create for comfort, and to avoid accepting responsibility for our own lives.

On one occasion, an emperor of Japan asked Rinzai if there was life after death. Rinzai said that he didn't know. "Then you should know", said the Emperor. "You're a Zen master". "Yes", confirmed Rinzai, "But not a dead one".

In Zen, two loosely formulated techniques are favoured for awakening consciousness. One is the hard way, the other is harder. In one, the Zen master intuitively chooses the precise instant in which to 'hit' in such a way that the novice's monkey mind is surprised out of the trap that it has set for itself. The Soto school favours intensive relaxation and the focusing of the eventually stilled mind single-pointedly on Zen koans. Koans are stories or riddles which appear utterly nonsensical to the intellectual or superficial mind: "Mounting seven steps, which leg does a stork use first?" "In clapping both hands, a sound is heard. What is the sound of the one hand?" "Show me your original face before your mother was born". "Pass me a stick with one end". The koans become increasingly obscure, but lead eventually to a deepening of perception and a fine-tuning of the intuitive and creative levels of consciousness. The two Zen techniques parallel, at another level, those available to the master hypnotist. Depending upon his carefully developed intuitive assessment of the real needs and capabilities of the subject, the master hypnotist can vary his approach to awaken various levels of consciousness either gradually or instantaneously. As with Zen, the transformation and awakening from a lifetime of self-delusion and deception can come as a shock. When the veil lifts and you awaken to realisation of how much depends on you, of the immensity of your personal power to hurt or to heal yourself and those around you, you can literally be shaken to the roots. Everything is different when you fully accept who is solely responsible for where you are now.

Zen originated in China as an offshoot of Buddhism, which itself is not strictly a religion, as any concept of divinity is again seen to be outside the scope of mortal mind. Rather it is seen as further evidence of the confused egocentric nature of Man, maintaining the illusion of his dominance by creating deities in his own image. One of the greatest contributions Buddha made to the spiritual evolution of mankind was his assurance that enlightenment, attainment of Buddha-mind, is accessible to all mankind. As he repeatedly demonstrated, it is in this sense that we are all created equal.

Krishnamurti, a latter-day enlightened Master, was chosen

"Tea up, Baba Ram."

for the equivalent of Messianic training at the age of fourteen, in the same way that the Essenes chose twenty-five youths for training in the Israelite Messianic tradition over a period of seven hundred years. He was selected because he still retained the virgin mind of a child. With an innocent mind, much time is saved. Before maturity, before sexual urges become a mental distraction, natural sex energy can be diverted and transformed into intense meditation and deep spiritual awareness. Krishnamurti was in fact so selfless, so unconscious of his separate identity, that his early teachers saw him as dim-witted, and people to whom he was presented in England dismissed him as simple-minded. Krishnamurti became the modern world's greatest Master in understanding how to awaken the most brilliantly intellectual and egocentric minds. His basic message: drop the mind, seek freedom from the known. The more powerful the man and the more intellectually conditioned his mind, the more difficult it is to convey that this is the way to fulfilment and a true understanding of life. The catch is that a master can only lead you to the edge of the deep chasm that separates conditioning and consciousness. There is no bridge. Drop conditioning, you can make the jump. You will find no need for conditioned thinking on the other side.

Meditation on light has been featured, in one way or another, in every religious and spiritual concept throughout the ages, as all men have long recognised and appreciated the life-giving energies derived from sunlight.

Yet there are deeper reasons than this, because you will soon find that whenever you meditate on light, or internalise it in practising hypnosis, something within you responds in the same way that a bud responds to sunlight. And the more you feel yourself moving into tune with light, the more apparent the beneficial influences become. A powerful and immediately accessible healing force awakens within you.

You may occasionally have heard the phrase 'You can convince yourself of anything', used in a derisory sense about a habitual worrier. You can prove for yourself that the statement is equally true in the positive sense. At least once a day, visualise light, get in tune with it, mentally bathe in it. And send it forth to people and places you know. You will find that it has an additional beneficial effect. It reflects back on the sender.

The Hermetic code, referred to earlier, conveys the interrelationships of all knowable kingdoms by reference to the Rule of Seven which, amongst other things, governs our sense or conception of sound and colour. It serves to indicate some of the limitations in perception of the human mind.

The basic kingdom, equivalent to the 'Do' sound in the musical scale, the first of the seven, is the mineral kingdom. The mineral kingdom serves each of the next three, the vegetable, animal and human kingdoms, and is also part of the fifth, the planetary kingdom. Next in ascendancy is the cosmic or universal kingdom and the seventh is the Supra-Universal, the All-in-All, the 'that which permeates, activates and embraces all the Universes'. The All-in-All then becomes the step before the number one or 'Do' of the next seven kingdoms, in an infinitely ascending series of scales which, like ultra-sonic sound frequencies and ultra-violet light, are beyond the scope of ordinary human perception.

The comments in this chapter only brush shoulders with the various topics which can be researched in depth by anyone so inclined. They are provided for those who can spare an occasional glance for the landscape that lies on either side of the path. Don't let the scenery distract you unduly. Walking the path is more important than knowing all about it. There is a Sufi story which illustrates this point in characteristic style. One day, a scholarly Sufi was wandering near a small lake, when he heard a dervish giving vent to ritual calls. The sound carried across the water from a small island. Both in the words and the intonation, the performance was hopelessly wrong. Borrowing a boat, the Sufi elder rowed to the island, found the young dervish and spent half-an-hour explaining his mistakes. The young man was deeply grateful. Half-way back to the mainland, the Sufi was startled to hear a 'splash, splash, splash' sound drawing nearer. It was the young dervish, running. He skidded to a halt alongside the boat. "Forgive me for delaying you, good friend", he panted. "You were quite right ... I am a complete idiot. What was that last line again?"

Stress check and relax. Realise that it is not the quantity of air you inhale but the quality that counts. Charge the air around you with electro-magnetic ions generated by positive thoughts. Imagine that, with the air you draw in love, light, life, health, wealth and harmony. Feel it, dedicate to it, not as doggerel but as your reality. The positive influences will strengthen every day. Use it at night before you sleep and enjoy the effect on your dreams.

"This merry mosaic of fumbles, follies, frolics and fun", mouthed Will Shakespeare, "That's plain brilliant, that is." "Pure genius", corrected Hakuin, applauding ecstatically with one giant hand.

Hypnotic sleep tapes

"There are few more impressive sights in the world than a Scotsman on the make". (Sir James Barrie)

This is where the story gets personal.

My own quest to understand more about the powers of mind really accelerated in the 1960's, when I attended an intensive training course on behavioural science in California, later becoming an instructor. Still later, in twenty or so countries throughout America, Africa, Europe and the Orient, I found opportunities to expand my understanding of hypnosis and kindred skills, applying them to personal health problems and financial management and marketing operations, all with noteworthy and occasionally spectacular results. Participating in a course on professional hypnotherapy presented by Barrie Konicov, recognised in the USA and elsewhere as a leader in the field, I became interested in the possibility of introducing translations of his self-hypnosis cassette tapes to Spain.

Before introducing twelve of the Konicov tapes in Spanish in 1983, I thoroughly tested, reviewed and analysed each one. Since then, I have studied a further forty of his tapes on subjects ranging from coping with fears, allergies and drug abuse to developing psychic healing skills and excelling at games and sport. The more I tested the more I became impressed with the masterly display of subject knowledge and hypnotic techniques. Their influence can only be beneficial. Subsequent experience with people who have used them has strengthened my early impressions.

It is always refreshing to have one's views confirmed by impartial and independent third parties. This confirmation was provided by a panel chosen by the health magazine *Yoga Today*. They reviewed no less than fourteen relaxation tapes which are available in the United Kingdom today. The Konicov tape was the only one awarded top marks, the remainder scoring from thirty to eighty-per-cent. The panel's report on the Konicov tape included the following comment:

'The tape was approved wholeheartedly by every member of the panel. This almost lyrical recording first promoted heightened awareness followed by deep relaxation.'

The article in the yoga magazine prompted me to review personally the competitive tapes which the yoga panel evaluated in the seventy to eighty per cent range. With one exception, I felt that the panel had been overly generous. Only one of the tapes illustrated a thorough understanding of hypnosis, but even in this recording the techniques used were outdated a decade ago.

The exception was a yoga exercise and relaxation tape which was so outstandingly worthwhile that it is included in the list of recommended tapes at the end of this book. The review I made of the British hypnotic tape offerings prompted me to introduce my own recordings in which the techniques learned from Barrie Konicov and other modern masters of hypnotherapy are featured.

Using the same rating system for hypnotic and yoga recordings seems unfair, as achieving a deep state of relaxation while performing conscious physical exercise is clearly difficult, if not impossible. Relaxing with self-hypnosis requires little movement other than unfurrowing your brow; in fact, the aim is to ensure that no energy is expended in unnecessary mental, physical or emotional activities. Should physical activity seem to be required, for example, in treating dislocations and postural problems, the subconscious control mind is simply directed to carry out the necessary 'manipulations'. No conscious effort is required. The control levels will initiate the necessary muscle movements automatically, effortlessly and without causing pain or damage through using excessive corrective force. The aim of the subconscious mind is always lifewards.

With extensive experience and practice, virtually complete control of the autonomic nervous system which, in turn, controls all life-sustaining bodily functions, is achievable with hypnosis and also with meditation techniques .... simply by relaxing and simplifying yourself.

The main advantage offered by the tape cassette recordings is that extensive experience and long hours of daily practice are not required. They truly offer the lazy pilgrim's guide to enlightenment. Whether you choose to relax the mind with muscle or relax the muscles with mind, the result is the same. A profound dynamism of the self is reawakened and life is seen from a more interesting vantage point, opening the way to still greater things, not only to develop and mature, but to excel and inspire.

Take five minutes right now to check your state of mind. Relax, centre, become calm and fully in control. Check to what extent you can ignore all mental signals which intefere with your decision to sit and do absolutely nothing for five minutes. If the static persists, focus on breathing more deeply but comfortably, silently, silently... Do this now.

If your head sounds like Piccadilly Circus on a Saturday night, use a relaxation tape. When you control your thoughts, you control your feelings. When you control your feelings, you control your destiny.

Hypnotic and accelerated learning tapes

Two types of Konicov tapes are available, self-hypnotic and subliminal persuasion. All tapes are carefully designed to deal with specific or general human needs and problems. Subliminal tapes, both cassette and video, feature the same beneficial messages as the hypnotic sleep tapes. A shorter day-version is usually provided on the second side of the hypnotic tapes. The sleep version provides up to forty-five minutes recording, with wake-up instructions for day use which the subconscious mind will ignore if the message is being played at bedtime.

Subliminal tapes: how they work

Subliminal tapes convey beneficial messages directly to the subconscious, avoiding any misinterpretation or editing by an overly critical, analytical, argumentative or otherwise negatively programmed conscious mind. The sound of waves or soft music is used to mask the messages, which are conveyed below the sonic range audible to the conscious mind.

The advantage with subliminal persuasion tapes is that they can be played while driving, as alertness at all levels of consciousness is greatly enhanced. You would be misled in thinking that you can sleep to the soothing sound of the waves: the underlying message keeps the mind fully alert.

Despite the beneficial nature of the messages, the tapes should never be used to influence the behaviour of other people without their full understanding and assent.

This naturally raises the question about the possibility of being subjected to subliminal persuasion without your knowledge and consent. If the messages are clearly beneficial and in tune with your personal needs and desires, they will normally be accepted by the subconscious. In this case, and even more so if the subliminal message does not meet these requirements or is distinctly negative, the subconscious will telegraph a clear warning signal, if you have daily attuned your awareness by practising the simple self-hypnotic techniques for shielding yourself against negative influences. Similarly, the subconscious will warn you if it is subjected to a subliminal message in a persuasive tone of voice which again is not in harmony with your normal thought patterns or habits. The warning signal is quite distinctive: your head hurts, as though you were exposed to discordant music.

Subliminal persuasion, either visual or vocal, is no longer pemitted in advertising, but it is, by its nature, clearly difficult to detect or prove. Like laser beams, the technique can be used constructively or destructively, depending upon the intention of the user.

A televised milk commercial recently featured in Britain used a less widely known hypnotic technique called double-induction. The method is simple and seems inoffensive, though sometimes irritating, as two voices at different tonal levels overlap or speak simultaneously. The lower-toned message speaks directly to the subconscious and unless it is negated, produces a strong motivational urge on the listener.

The effect of conveying differently worded messages to the conscious and subconscious levels of mind is divisive and can have a negative influence on health. If, for some reason, you are exposed to this technique and are unable to switch off the sound physically, immediately relax and give the auto-suggestion to 'negate all audible messages except my voice, now', until such time as the double-induction exposure ceases. If you become aware of any unwanted changes in your habit patterns, give the appropriate mental instructions for eliminating them.

An indication of the influence of subliminal messages was provided by reports in the *Wall Street Journal* and *Time* magazine of tests in a supermarket and a departmental store. Messages were piped through the public address system, masked by incidental music. The messages ... 'I take pride in being honest. I do not steal' ... resulted in a significant reduction in pilferage. Against a customary upwards trend in shop-lifting losses, the department store recorded a thirty-seven-per-cent reduction over a period of nine months.

Choosing a hypnotic tape

A list of recommended cassette tapes is provided at the end of the book. The 'Good Health' tape covers general health problems. It induces a relaxed state of mind, enabling carefully chosen positive suggestions to be conveyed directly to the subconscious.

Since at least eighty-per-cent of all physical and psychological problems are now recognised to be stress-related, one of the major benefits provided by every tape is the reduction of stress levels in both mind and body. There is no situation in which this is not a major contributing factor to health improvement, as all levels of consciousness are brought into harmony, resulting in improved functioning of the autonomic processes, which include heart beat, blood pressure, pain management, healing and other vital physiological functions.

Despite the wide range of general and specific subjects covered by the recordings, there may be some which are not presently provided. This eventuality is covered by the 'Self-Hypnosis' tape, which provides all the information required to enable a person to convey uniquely personal positive suggestions to the mind. Instruction is also given for preparing suggestions for change in the precise form necessary to ensure their acceptance and prompt implementation.

Apart from the tapes on specific health problems, there are many subjects which require special knowledge and experience to ensure that the required auto-suggestions are correctly phrased for maximum effectiveness. Memory training, taking examinations, creative writing, salesmanship, handling criticism, decision-making and coping with unemployment are some of the extensive range of recordings available.

For every subject covered by the tapes, years of professional hypnotherapy experience and thousands of case histories have contributed to determining the probable negative thought patterns which are the hidden cause of every problem or lack. On the basis of this information, meticulously worded suggestions are selected to uncover the negative influence and replace it with fresh, positive thought patterns, freeing the system permanently from the hidden handicap.

Your experience with one recording will make your progress with other subjects easier. For best results, work on one subject at a time. An exception to this is that the self-healing and self-hypnosis tapes may be used effectively with any other subject.

For anyone in a highly emotional state of mind the relaxation tape is recommended. Other tapes including self-hypnosis and self-healing should not be used until a relaxed state of mind is achieved through using the relaxation recording.

Even if you are perfectly satisfied with your state of health, you will greatly benefit from listening to the self-healing tape. Apart from other practical influences, you will find that your understanding of other people's attitudes and aspirations is greatly enhanced in a way that cannot be conveyed in writing.

Success with any subject may come with the very first playing, or it may require daily playings for thirty or more days. Success depends entirely on two factors: the degree to which you learn to relax completely, and the extent to which negative conditioning in the past is inhibiting achievement of your present desires.

With every tape your success is guaranteed, simply because within each of us is the seed of unlimited personal power and positive potential. The function of the tape is to stimulate your unlimited potential by bringing your conscious desires and your subconscious yearnings into harmony and balance. When this is achieved anything worthwhile in life is effortlessly attainable.

There is in fact a refreshing growth in the incidence of patients being weaned off prescriptions for tranquilisers by offering them self-hypnosis relaxation tapes as an alternative. There are no unwelcome side effects or dependency problems with self-hypnosis cassettes and the results are usually encouraging, despite the fact that withdrawal from the use and abuse of tranquilisers can be as much as ten times more difficult than withdrawal from the notorious and addictive 'hard' drugs.

The use of psychoactive drugs as tranquilisers mushroomed from the mental hospitals into the community at large. Their use is defended on the grounds that there is no risk of irreversible side effects as long as they are correctly prescribed.

The professional hypnotist

"The universe is full of magical things, patiently waiting for our wits to grow sharper." (Eden Phillpotts)

There are fifty levels of hypnosis identified on the LECRON-BORDEAUX scale, from the state of simple physical relaxation — the 'stress check' — to the deepest level of plenary trance. Taped hypnosis techniques are designed to induce a light level of hypnotic trance up to stage eighteen. Depending on several factors — the skill of the hypnotist, the capability and motivation of the subject, and the content of the particular hypnotic material, beneficial influences are induced from the tenth level, which is marked by slower and deeper breathing and a slower pulse rate. The fifth level is adequate for many purposes. This is the state of mental relaxation which is experienced when we daydream. With practice, deeper levels of relaxation can be experienced, but these are not required for conveying positive suggestions of change to the subconscious.

Popular misconceptions.... the professional hypnotist..

Apart from professional instruction courses for doctors, dentists and other health-care specialists, skilled hypnotherapists are experienced in several highly effective techniques used in diagnosis and in other special circumstances. These procedures require an uncommonly high level of sensitivity, dedication and skill, which cannot presently be conveyed in recordings.

Due to their calling, hypnotists are more aware than most people of the extent of the positive and negative power available to the human mind, and particularly of the grave danger to the hypnotist or any other person who seeks to impose his will on another.

The understanding and positive self-control which a master hypnotist first learns to apply to his own lifestyle ensures that he is one of the most conscientious people you are ever likely to meet.

The management of pain

Those unfortunates who live with pain for a long time tend to develop an overall negative attitude, and it is always something of a miracle to find that they can still be awakened to a more positive outlook on life.

Just as torchlight instantly dispels darkness which has ruled in a cavern for years, self-hypnosis can disperse a lifetime's accumulation of negative conditioning. This, whether the habitual sufferer approaches the subject through mild curiosity or with the thought that there is nothing much to lose. Either way, the healing process starts on hearing the hypnotic message for the first time.

One of the best ways to encourage a negative reaction to hypnotism is to insist that a problem is all in the mind. This is one monkey mind talking to another, and you know how useless that is.

The initial difficulty is that, to people who have absorbed heavy negative programming, anything easy will seem too good to be true. Faced with a positive concept they become lost in their own questions — like: 'with self-hypnosis, are you telling me we can live forever?' Not so, but you can at least choose a better option than entertaining pain as a lifelong companion. Certainly it is never too late to learn, but why postpone learning until your negligence has limited your options to suppressing pain and achieving peace of mind? The sooner you see that your way of life is strictly what you choose it to be, the sooner you can choose to influence the time and manner of your death. Your consciousness has been given to you to use.

It can be helpful to direct a sufferer's questioning mind to his own beliefs, religious and otherwise. How many of them are better classified as superstitions? Have they been tested for sense? Have they enriched his life in any way? Is it possible that we are not really misfits in this Garden of Eden planet? That we have acquired or have been given powers to apply in this lifetime which, through generations of ignorance and neglect have become hidden from ourselves like some kind of mental lost property? Through lack of awareness, can we be cheating ourselves out of life? Even with ninety-per-cent awareness, are we not still potential victims ten-per-cent of the time?

Why, if we feel the need to believe in something, do we find it so difficult to start by believing in ourselves? Start that way, then perhaps we can find out why it's a good idea. Have you ever thought about developing your imagination, or do you see that as the sole province of science fiction writers and advertising agents? You can start with a familiar exercise: go for a holiday in your imagination; daydream a little. Choose your favourite place or invent one. Make it the kind of day when it feels just great to loll about and do absolutely nothing. Choose solitude or a happy holiday scene and be there enjoying every minute of it. You know that you can go on a mental holiday anytime you feel the need. See the point ... you can choose how to use your imagination ... to feel how you choose to feel. With practice, it becomes easier and more realistic every time. The holiday feeling becomes a habit. A healthy habit.

What you feel most of time — what you feel, not what you think — becomes your reality. That's the way the subconscious works. It makes real what you feel, it's as simple as that. With relaxation, you create a neutral zone in which positive feelings can blossom, and this reflects in your whole being. Your creative imagination creates.

Kidding ourselves? Fine. So you, who play that dreary game of always nearly dying, why not kid yourself alive? There's no cosmic bogeyman spying on you and making you pay in pain for your petty indiscretions. You're doing it all to yourself. You are paying for your lack of consciousness.

There is ample evidence that early childhood experiences can influence your adult life. As a young child you were entirely dependent on your parents for survival. You needed assurance of their love and a feeling of security. To the degree that their love was withheld or your sense of security was weakened by their occasional bickering and worry sessions, you grew up seeking compensations, and you will have found none. For the love of a mother and the understanding and firm guidance of a father there are no later substitutes. With self-hypnosis techniques, you learn to accept that, though you were denied a one-time necessity, you can now understand and forgive your parents and cease seeking substitutes for something you no longer need. Then, and only then, are you on the way to finding peace of mind and maturity as an adult.

The same pattern can be repeated at later stages of life. A sense of lack or rejection, imagined or real, can subconsciously influence your attitudes and actions and compensations will be sought through alchohol, drugs and tranquillisers. Or you will fall for one or more of the other compensatory traps, seeking attention through accidents or illnesses, or perhaps dedicating your life to amassing a fortune and then choosing to live in poverty as a recluse, still seeking in vain for mental peace. A truly enlightened person, it should be mentioned, never seeks to hide or retire from everyday life. With his enhanced awareness of what this planet offers, he lives every moment of his life to the full.

To awaken a dedicated sufferer to the deep-rooted causes of a prolonged illness, a professional hypnotherapist will normally recommend an age-regression technique. This is a highly effective method of eliminating both the problem and the symptoms within less than an hour, but it cannot yet be conveyed as a self-hypnotic technique. This will have to await the development of talk-back home computers.

The hypnotist will normally insist on conducting the session in the presence of an assistant or the sufferer's medical adviser, rather than a friend or relative. This is to avoid embarrassing a companion who may learn, during the course of the session, that he has been unwittingly contributing to the sufferer's unhealthy state of mind.

It may seem miraculous that a dramatic transformation can occur in a matter of minutes and, in a way, it is. Have you seen what a sprinkling of rain can do to a desert? There is an instant rebirth, and the effect of the age-regression technique is exactly the same.

Long-term sufferers are prone to physical discomfort and a level of pain which can inhibit attempts to relax. This is provided for in the appropriate tapes, which include a caution that the indirect pain elimination technique which is given should never be used to mask other conditions which may require to be diagnosed by a competent physician.

Occasions may arise when a more direct pain relief method is required, for example, when the effect of pain relieving chemicals has diminished due to prolonged use. A hypnotherapist will be prepared to demonstrate the technique on the recommendation of a qualified medical practitioner.

Anybody who has acquired some prior experience of self-hypnosis can learn to apply this additional technique in less than an hour. The recommended practice is to remove the pain for a period of no more than twenty-four hours, repeating the simple procedure daily as many times as necessary.

The next step is then to use relaxation techniques to identify the cause. You have been holding onto your pain for a reason. When you see the reason, the pain drops away. It will not return.

There has never been anything mystical or magical about the elimination of pain and disease through hypnosis. The ability to relax and focus the power of your imagination is all that has ever been required. When you have mastered this technique you will find that it does not mark the end of the story, but a new beginning.

For there is a natural law which is apparent to anyone who can see beyond the screen of the superficial, which often turns out to be a cunning disguise. In the long run, love, peace, health and harmony will prevail.

The meaning of dream messages

"His life was a sort of dream, as are most lives with the mainspring left out." (F. Scott Fitzgerald)

The advantage of knowing how to decipher your own dreams, particularly those that are persistent and repetitive, is that you can rapidly remove blockages in the mental system which are causing confusion at the subconscious levels of mind.

The various types of dream have been categorised, but this proves to be more of a hindrance than a help, because you, and only you, can experience the 'Ah-ha' moment when the full meaning of the dream message becomes abundantly clear. Despite all the literature available on the subject, dreams cannot be accurately analysed by reference to the experience of other people with apparently identical dreams. When you have applied the self-hypnosis interpretation technique you will see why.

All dreams contain some sort of message. One which is constantly repeating, whether as a dream or nightmare, as a 'good' or 'bad' dream, is clear evidence of the existence of a disturbing or disruptive influence at the subconscious levels, which the conscious mind is either choosing to ignore or is incapable of removing.

In sleep, or relaxed and centered, we enter more into touch with our other half, the half which returns, with every vibration, from our manifested physical state of being to the energy source from which our being springs. It is at this level of existence that mystics refer to everything as being 'One'. Because of the persistence of the subconscious in sending the picture-message and consequently our better conscious recollection of it, we can more readily help to bring the meaning to the surface.

The clarification technique brings together several of the skills we develop in practising self-hypnosis: relaxing, imaging and expanding our awareness.

Imaging, in this context, involves more than seeing the other person or thing in the mind's eye. We require to transfer ourselves to the other, becoming the other in our imagination and responding to questions as we imagine the other might respond. As with other hypnotic exercises, to the extent that we can enter into the spirit of what, intellectually, we may regard as a childish game, the subconscious levels awaken to the fact that something new is happening, a new channel is being provided, and they respond by adjusting themselves to use it.

Three further points need to be mentioned. Firstly, this is definitely not a childish game. Childlike, yes. It would normally be essential to warn a neurotic or a deeply distressed or nervous person not to attempt the exercise, but such a person would, in any case, fail to achieve the states of relaxation and relationship necessary to start.

Secondly, we need to remember that the subconscious levels, from which dreams arise, are prone to mix the time sequence of recent and earlier events. Future events are also telegraphed, but until our awareness is sharpened, we fail to see that we are being helped in this way. We are often pre-warned, not necessarily to the extent that a future event will not happen, but to enable us, through our heightened awareness, to minimise or even completely avoid the negative mental or physical effect on us which could otherwise have had more serious consequences. At one time, presumably, premonition skills and our 'sixth sense' were readily accessible to all of us.

Finally, you will require to accept that everything and everybody in a dream is you. This does not mean that if you dream of a mouse wearing a helmet that you yourself are timid or mouselike and need to protect your head. It means that if you can playact the role of the mouse or the tin hat in the dream, as though the dream were actually happening, then the channel opens and the meaning of the dream message becomes crystal clear.

To convey the concept, an outline of the procedure will be given next, followed by two actual case studies.

1. Recall a recent dream. You may find that you have to make a written note of tomorrow's dream on awakening.

2. Relax, centre to a light level of hypnosis.

3. Revive and relive the events of the dream in the present tense. Re-enter the spirit of the dream, be in the moment: 'I'm on a beach, a sandy beach. There's a rock here, a wet rock with a large book on it. I'm going to read it when ... etc'. You may only recall a fragment of the dream. This is fine. The more you recapture the feeling of it, the more you will find you can recall.

4. Be one of the characters or things in the dream. And be yourself, talking to it. Give the 'thing' a human mind, a human consciousness. 'Ham' it up, for example: 'Are you happy as a book?' 'Sure, I'm very useful and people appreciate me'.

'Why are you sitting on a wet rock?' 'Someone left me here. I think they forgot'. And so on ...

Continue ham-acting the two parts, you and it, as though you had just met someone interesting who was prepared to answer a lot of personal questions about himself. Respond, in this case, as you might imagine a humanform book might respond. It's your dream.

Realise that talking to ourselves is nothing new: thinking is sub-vocal conversation with ourselves and, sadly, we are doing this most of the time.

Here are a few examples of the kind of questions which can prompt the 'other party' to respond spontaneously and sincerely:

Are you happy as a ....? (type of person or thing)

Do you like being used that way?

Would you rather be somebody/something else?

What is your purpose in life?

Do you get any fun out of living?

What do you think of people in general?

What would you really like to be?

Are you happy as you are?

Can I do anything to help you?

What do you know about me?

Ask any question that springs to mind, no matter how irrelevant or ridiculous it may seem. Often, the response that you are prompted to give is the one that rings all the bells and wins the coconut.

If, after asking and responding to three or four questions, no bells toll, relive the dream again but choose a different person or thing and really get into it as a question and answer session in real life. The more unusual the character or the nature of the object you choose, the easier it is to allow the imagination to write the script. Sometimes just one question and answer brings the 'Ah-ha' moment, the realisation of the truth. On occasion, you may find it pays to stay with one 'personality', changing the pattern of questions and answers. Bathtime can provide an excellent opportunity for relaxing and practising the technique.

Complete each session with a stress check, relax and be grateful. It will be even easier next time.

In your responses, you will suddenly use a phrase that rings a bell at all levels of your being: head, heart and stomach. There is no possibility of mistaking the message: it is a bitter-sweet experience, an enlightening blend of sadness and gladness, as you realise how blind you have been to something that has really been staring you in the face. Note it down, because the monkey mind will want you to forget it again. Refresh your memory by reading your notes every few months.

If there is no 'Ah-ha' moment, patience. The channel will open, it may need a little more time to see what you are aiming to do. If you think that you can see what the message is but you have no strong bitter-sweet reaction, ignore it. The monkey is still playing tricks. Work on your next dream and get a really animated chat going with a kerbstone, a three-legged gnome or whatever else presents itself to play its part.

Two actual cases should suffice to convey sufficient detail for you to develop the technique. They are slightly condensed versions. The first exercise was only successful when three different approaches were tried.

The person involved was an American working on an assignment as a senior executive in an Australian company, reporting to the controlling corporation in New York and to the local managing director. It was a lonely assignment.

The dream: 'I am a large white cat. I'm sitting on top of a wall. Something whizzes over my head. A boy is below, firing at me. I jump off and float to the ground, unhurt.'

Ham-acting the part of the 'human' cat:

What are you doing sitting on the wall?

"Resting, I suppose. I just found myself here."

Why are you being fired at?

"How should I know? I'm doing no harm. Perhaps it's just ... because ... I'm here!!!" ... which triggered the 'Ah-ha' moment.

Some hours later, the executive was with the managing director when he exploded in anger over a report the executive was required to send to his vice-president in New York, copying the managing director, Jack. The managing director became personally offensive.

"A moment, Jack ... are you annoyed with me as a person, or do you just resent the fact that the Corporation wants to have a representative here? Is it me or just because I'm here?"

Jack cooled down immediately, confirmed his respect and friendship, and together they agreed a way of reporting jointly, which the New York office accepted.

Some weeks later, the same executive had a dream message which prompted him to take exceptional action in covering debts due in America dollars. The action saved A$200,000, when the Australian dollar unexpectedly devalued by twelve-per-cent. Currency experts worldwide were caught unawares, because all financial indicators pointed to a still stronger Australian dollar. The controlling company and the local board of directors said they thoroughly understood when the executive told them that he would prefer not to have to reveal the confidential source of his information.

In the second case, the subject was a highly successful South American businessman, married to an American girl. He found that his wife's understanding of him fell far short of his mother's, which they both recognised was the reason for a rapidly deteriorating relationship.

Manuel could only recall part of the dream, but it was repetitive and vivid: "I'm in the courtyard of the family home. The courtyard is paved with cobblestones and it's raining."

The dialogue: How do you like life as a cobblestone? Fine. I'm warm and smooth and strong. Now its starting to rain, how does that feel? Great. The water's warm. I feel it flowing over me now, flowing under the huge mahogany door that leads on to the town square, the plaza, flowing ...OUT ...

That was it, the 'Ah-ha' moment, bitter-sweet, laughing-crying, the laughing apparently hurting more than the sobbing.

Manuel explained: "We have always been wealthy. I was tutored, never went to schools or colleges. 'Outside' to me meant the courtyard: I was never allowed to go out and mix with the village children, after all, they were only peasants, as mother used to say. I could often hear the other children laughing and playing games on the other side of the door ... I longed to join them. My mother was never my friend! She never understood me as a child. I grew up with old people ... I was her prisoner!"

Exit the false image of an understanding mother. Exit the division in Don Manuel's mind. When we are divided in ourselves, we are divided from everyone. The mind can never be at peace with itself. Once the interpretative channel is established, there is sometimes a tendency for the subconscious levels to become over-stimulated, to the extent that messages are poured forth about blockages which have perhaps existed for years. Back off for a while, slow the whole process down by ignoring dreams for several days at a time. The mirror of the mind shows you clearly what you are, which is never what you think you are. A little truth at a time is quite enough. Your friends and companions need more time to adjust to the new you than you need to adjust to yourself. Now that the channel is established, you will not lose access to it, you can be sure of that.

The second point is more general advice: don't get involved with or attached to this technique or any other. Attachment to anything, whether to a person, system, religion, ideal or a hypnotic technique is certain evidence of immaturity and lack of understanding. They can all provide temporary diversion or comfort, as a teddy bear or a fairy tale does for a child. They can serve some purpose at specific stages of growth and development.

Dick Alpert, a one-time professor of psychology at Harvard University, suggests that if you feel the need for attachment, choose an ice-cream cone. That way, you will learn sooner to come to rely on yourself. Because living is an on-going experience, learn all you can from each fairy story, then discard it and stride on. There is always more adventure ahead, more to be understood or wondered at, more living experience to enjoy.

Progress with dream interpretation, linked to the daily elimination of negative influences using self-hypnotic techniques, normally follows a similar pattern:

- The subconscious prompts the playacting more directly, suggesting the questions and answers which reveal the sense of the dream message.

- Gradually, you become more conscious, during your dreams, that you are, in fact, dreaming.

- The dream messages cease to be distorted. They become more and more plainly expressed and simple to understand.

- Everyday awareness becomes fine-tuned to the extent that dream messages are no longer required.

At any one of these stages, you may notice an improvement in your powers of ESP, in precognition. Be grateful and ... be discreet.

With all levels of mind in harmony, the need for a nightly unravelling process ceases. Your sleep will be blissful, refreshing, healthy, like the sleep of a happy child who knows only the comfort of selfless love.

The younger ones

"A gifted small girl has explained that pins are a great way of saving life, 'by not swallowing them'".(C.E. Montague)

Every new generation understandably brings a new wave of revolt against the older ways. Intuitively, the younger generation see that the prevailing lifestyle has nothing much to offer them. With at least eighty-per-cent of the population unhappy in their work, aware only that they are caught in something that they have failed to take the trouble to understand, no great depth of intuition is required to see the pointlessness of it all. Children of all cultures and classes grow up in houses of ill dispute. Their revolt takes every imaginable form of expression, from flowering cactus hair styles to accessories more appropriate for circus horses. The inevitable yin-yang pendulum swing widens as stress and desperation increase. A new form of slavery spreads to meet the frenetic need for generating the negative energy required: the drug culture thrives and a mental parasite takes the place of ice-cream. Since the introduction of tapes which can release addicts from the physical, mental and emotional dependency on drugs, more have been sold in Britain than the formerly most popular duo, 'Weight Reduction' and 'Stop Smoking'.

Part of our parental responsibility is to provide a 'safe house' for a child to grow up in, a home in which the child can always find understanding, that deepest form of unselfish love. With that understanding must come the realization that seeking security in the world is a futile pursuit: living with insecurity is perhaps the only lesson we are here to learn.

The range of Konicov tapes includes subjects which contribute to the development of sound personality and character in people of all ages, from ten to eighty, and several are specifically for children. When you select a tape for a young child, whatever the subject — nail-biting, hyperactivity, parental animosity etc. — listen to it yourself, consciously, not when you are tired. The important contributions you can make to resolving the child's problem will be revealed to you. Both of you will benefit from this understanding, of that you can be sure. The greatest help we can give anyone, including our children, is learning to understand ourselves.

Sadly, many people marry long before they have learned to live happily with themselves, without diversions and other forms of external support. They bring their confusion, insecurity and unhappiness to the wedding to complement their partner's conscious and subconscious problems.

Each and every one of us is an original being, unique, distinctive. No child is intended to be a carbon copy of a parent. If we only teach our children to imitate, we should not be upset later to see them imitate whatever lunatic trend is in vogue. By expanding our own understanding, we can generate the kind of atmosphere in which the child's original-ity can blossom, free from doubts, fears, superstitions and other nonsenses which inhibited or warped our own develop-ment.

This way we can break the chain of negative events, so that the sins of the parents cease to be visited on the children unto the third and fourth generation. Your child can become one of the first of a new generation of humans, more worthy of their being.

There has never been a need for any of us to prove our individuality, the gift of life is proof enough. Each one of us is a living, breathing miracle, a Child of the Universe, born to experience the incredible joy of living in harmony with ourselves and nature, guided, supported and sustained by the love and the light of the spirit within us.

Declaration of interdependence

'Do not expect to drive pain away by pretending it is unreal. Pain, if you seek serenity in Oneness, vanishes of its own accord.' (Sengstan Buddhist texts)

As a child, you may never have experienced the frustration of finding that you can't bring part of a wave home in a sand bucket. If you have had this kind of experience and wish to relive it, you can do so by attempting to capture the essence of the Hermetic Principles of Life in a few pages. So if you feel the urge for a deep and thorough understanding of how and why all kinds of forces, energies and substances yield to the domination of the emanations from the mind which we call thought waves, refer to 'The Kybalion'.

'The Kybalion' itself makes no claim to be other than a superficial review, but it does convey some of the brilliance. Thanks to physicists like Fritzof Capra (*'The Tao of Physics'*) it is fairly widely accepted that modern-day scientists, with access to cyclotrons and other electronic equipment, are now enabled to demonstrate what Hermes Trismegistus discovered centuries ago. What the Hermetic schools and their successors, the Essenes, Jain Teerthankeras and other esoteric groups have so far failed to do is convince Man that he is not only capable of determining his own destiny, but is responsible for determining the destiny of his own planet. We have allowed our consciousness to develop a distinctly negative bias: we only recognise that we have the power to destroy ourselves.

We can accept that Man is a unity of mind, spirit and body. We have learned to shine mentally and physically, but few have learned how to shine their spirit. In other words, we have developed two-thirds of the whole, the two easy parts. We are easily misled by myths and adult fairy tales. Despite the efforts of a few thousand 'whole' men to alert us to our folly, Man has allowed himself to become not so much mentally as spiritually retarded.

We can start to correct the imbalance by taking responsibility for ourselves. And we don't need a cyclotron to see if the Hermetic Principles make sense.

To avoid writing a detailed 'Initiation to Hermetism' which has already been done by Franz Bardon — at least in German and Spanish — these comments will be confined to summarising some of the principles which relate to mental unease and physical disease:

"In the material or phenomenal world, everything which falls within the limited range of our human senses is generally accepted to be a relatively temporary manifestation of 'Spirit' or 'Infinite Intelligence'. In other words, it is not so much an illusion created by whirling atoms as a temporary form of seemingly solidified thought."

In brief, if you will accept, subject to later experience, that beyond matter and energy is mind, and mind is all there is, you can take all of the theories and concepts of how the human condition works and make sense out of them all, as Barrie Konicov explains.

Further, "if our world of reality is a world of effect, not cause, whatever adverse physical condition you are faced with has to be a symptom, and the cause is always thought, your thought or thoughts. So the only requirement is to trace back to the event which triggered the mental reaction. Whatever the symptom, whatever the disease, removal of the thought will remove the problem."

So what influences the positive and negative energies of thought? Our thoughts about an event. Our personal control over the events in our lives may be greater than we realise, but for present purposes, let us assume that events just happen to us. Dozens of events happen daily, most of them quite trivial in nature. You find difficulty in parking your car. Someone bumps into you as you are crossing a street, and doesn't apologise. You find you have mislaid an important report. The events happen, that's all. How you react to them is what determines their effect on you.

So the sequence is first of all the event, then the thought followed by the emotional reaction. If you feel that you have been put upon in some way, or your position or person has been threatened or abused, you may react negatively with anger, hate, fear, worry or any one of a series of negative emotions. Make this kind of negative reaction a habit and your health will suffer to some degree or other. In this respect, like attracts like. You will actually attract more events which will trigger your negative responses. You may seek relief and find how to suppress the symptoms, but the root of the problem remains, more deeply established, growing in power.

Why is an event that upsets one person overlooked by another?

The more divided we are in ourselves, the more harshly we judge other people and events. Judging other people is easier than looking at ourselves. The Hermetic theory of polarity explains that all opposites are identical in nature but different in degree. This can be illustrated by drawing a line as follows:

COLD   HOT

∞   A _____ B   ∞

Each end of the line is represented as stretching out to infinity. With 'hot' at one end and 'cold' at the other, where would you mark the position of no heat, no cold? If 'A' represented 'mountain' and 'B' represented 'valley', where would the moutain start? Ponder good and bad, wet and dry, cheap and expensive. Nothing is absolute, all opposites are different only in degree, not in their nature. Towards the 'B' end of the line, it is less cold.

Your judgment is always biased by the very fact that it is a personal assessment and therefore unique. The same is the case for everyone else.

The temperature in a centrally-heated home, for example, may be too warm for you and too cold for your wife. Accept this and seek an equitable solution. Allow the matter to become a source of perpetual irritation and it will soon reflect in family health. Nagging, bickering and temper tantrums are the bugle calls of marital civil war and invariably symptomatic of the existence of deeper mental hurts, imagined or real, which need to be identified, understood and forgiven.

The same principle applies to dozens of mental polarities like right-wrong, generous-selfish, success-failure, secure-insecure, lie-truth, glad-sad. When love comes in, the certainty of 'less love' or 'more love' comes with it. All along the infinite line, there are hundreds of degrees of love. There is hate in love and love in hate. And it is this apparent paradox that enables the Hermetist to apply the law of polarity to transmute all negatives to positives, to higher vibrations, simply by bringing the positive thought-power of understanding into the picture.

So, the event is, now it is not. Someone has barged into you. Could you perhaps have been a little more alert? Was it intentional? He was unaware, didn't even notice that he had hit you. Perhaps he has just had some bad news. Anyway, send him love and light, he needs it at least as much as you do. Do it, you will feel the difference. Once you develop the habit, the ability to react positively becomes more and more natural to you. You attract more positive power. Lifeforce is an abundance, an overflowing of positive energies, always seeking a channel through which to flow. Provide the channel.

'Two reeds drink from one stream. One is hollow, the other is sugar cane.' (Jaluludin Rumi, *Sufi*)

If questions and doubts spring to your mind, brush them aside for the moment. Or write them down and refer back to them in a month's time. That way, you will learn something more about yourself that nobody else can tell you.

So it is not the event but how we choose to view the event which can cause disease. Let's take an example. Suppose, through no apparent fault of our own, we suffer severe physical injury, let's say the loss of a limb. It was not our own fault? We were just in the wrong place at the wrong time? These are both negative judgments with negative polarity and they bring further suffering into being. As simply as that.

Accept that the event is and that judgment of any kind can only give rise to negative feelings. This understanding is all that is needed to free the mind from negativity so that the natural process of healing is accelerated and no mental bruises are created, to take root and fester in the subconscious. For events that have occurred and have been judged in the past, centre, release them and forgive everybody involved, particularly yourself for the errors of thought and the erroneous interpretations.

What really happens when we judge events or others? Through our physical senses we become aware of an 'outside' stimulus or event: we feel, hear, see, smell or taste it. We also think about it and by doing so, we internalise a negative influence. The 'right action' is to recognise a particular thought as negative and reject it: you don't need it. As we grow in understanding of the vital interrelationship of all things, we find that, in judging something or somebody negatively, we only succeed in denying a part of ourselves.

'Inside' and 'outside' are quite arbitrary terms, having as little significance on the universal scale as up, down and sideways. Our individual minds, bodies and spirits are part of, and inseparable from, the mental, material and astral planes of the Universe. We are separate entities and, at the same time, an integral part of everything known and unknowable. We are subject, at the very least, to the perpetual influences of radiation, vibration, gravity, atmospheric pressure and polarity, all of which are, in common with all things, in a continuous state of ebbing and flowing, of cosmic dance and each of us is also influenced by gender and individual, racial and group consciousness. From what standpoint then, do we presume to judge anybody or anything? Is anyone capable of standing far enough back from it all to gain perspective, objectivity?

> *"What's done we partly may compute,*
> *But know not what's resisted."*

                                    (Robert Burns, 1759-1796)

Barrie Konicov illustrates the psychoanalytical theory of illness with the following diagram:

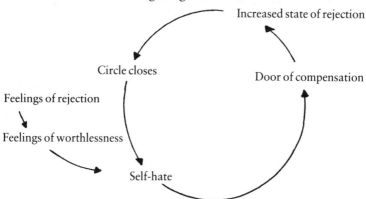

Briefly, three or more events are needed to trigger a disease condition. The later events are known to the conscious mind, the initial event is forgotten.

The first event, the 'Initial Sensitising Event', may be interpreted by us as a rebuff or rejection, even if no actual rebuff was intended. Once this interpretation is accepted, however, the other feelings follow — worthlessness, self-dislike, self-hate. This leads inevitably to attempts to escape from the self-negating feelings by choosing one or more forms of compensation. Pass through this door and our feelings of rejection become realities: we are rejected. Our personal sense of rejection increases and the vicious circle closes on itself.

The initial sensitising event is never enough, by itself, to create serious imbalance and disease. Usually at least two more events are required. The nature of the events can be quite dissimilar, but the mind interprets them as identical to the first and this compounds the initial emotional shock. Mild symptoms will surface after the second event and this stage is recalled by the conscious mind. The third event produces clearly visible symptoms of ill-health and the reactions pass out of all conscious control.

An explanation of the roles played by psychological antigens and antibodies is omitted here, to avoid detracting from the vital central theme, as identification of the disruptive thought patterns under hypnosis is all that is required to restart the process of correcting imbalance in all areas.

The initial event which creates an area of sensitivity in our being is often experienced in childhood. It could be the shock of finding that a parent can react explosively to some act which had no significance to us. Years later, an amorous rebuff or the unexpected loss of a job can ring the same bell and trigger the cellular imbalance that produces the symptoms and the disease.

The feelings of rejection, if taken to heart and not recognised as a negative reaction to a false image we have made of ourselves, can lead us to seek compensations, to hide from ourselves. These compensations can take any or several of the following easily recognisable forms:

- Drugs, alcohol, tranquillisers
- Psychosomatic escape — illness, accident proneness
- Overexertion — ego inflation, strenuous sport, business, politics, religious activities
- Crime — risks, negative energy stimulation
- Lunacy — neuroses, paranoia, seeing the world as alien
- Overeating, smoking, oral stimulation
- Cruelty, sadism, suicide
- Sexuality, animal behaviour

Any of these compensations indicates that, at some level, we dislike ourselves and are seeking a funkhole, a refuge in escape. We need help and the help we are likely to get is at the symptom level. Using self-hypnosis, preferably with an experienced professional or the appropriate tape, you can regress to the initial sensitising event, reinterpret it with understanding, changing its polarity and activating the positive mental force of forgiveness before returning to the present time.

Correction of the unhealthy state, no matter how apparently serious it seems, is not a question of calling for miracles. The cause is always negative thought: it is corrected immediately with understanding.

We can learn the wisdom of becoming entirely unreceptive to sensations arising from external forms, witnessing them, but not internalising them, not taking them to heart.

The more we learn to understand ourselves and our extra-ordinary powers, the more we can avoid becoming attached to illusions which we allow to hurt us when they collapse. We can do nothing to change the past but we can certainly learn to forgive and forget, to let bygones be bygones. Every moment is a new experience to be lived and enjoyed.

Students of Zen will remember the story of Zen master Nan Chan, who was walking through a village, accompanied by a Taoist monk, on the way to a monastery. It had been raining and the unpaved street was thick with mud. A young girl was standing on one side, undecided as to how to cross without spoiling her pretty shoes. Nan Chan bowed, picked the girl up and carried her across. She thanked him profusely. Nan Chan and the monk resumed their journey. After a meal in the monastery, the monk could restrain himself no longer. 'I always believed', he said, 'that Zen discipline was much stricter than ours. But a Taoist monk is not permitted to address a young female, let alone pick her up and carry her across a street.'

'I put her down some hours ago', replied Nan Chan. 'It seems that you are still carrying her on your back'.

"Who can offend the spirit? Can the firefly offend the stars?
Is the spirit a still pool that you can trouble with a staff?
This too concerns me deeply!......"

World consciousness

"To leave great themes unfinished is perhaps the most satisfying exercise of power." (George MacBeth)

Vibrant good health and prosperity are bonuses waiting to be claimed simply by understanding our interrelationship with the mental, spiritual and material influences which surround us. Aware of it or not, we are deeply intertwined at all these levels with all things and creatures great and small.

The rhythm of breathing is one of the more apparent links we have with the 'outside'. A simple change in the rhythm changes our consciousness, diminishing our 'exterior' awareness and freeing the mind momentarily. Relaxing, the deeper levels of consciousness merge into closer harmony, expanding and multiplying the powers of mind. This, in turn, allows the intuitive and creative levels to come fully into play, providing us with positive control over our lives and destinies.

All of us have sole personal responsibility for elevating our own level of consciousness. In doing so, we contribute to elevating the consciousness of the entire human race. Everyone who leaves the responsibility to someone else is choosing to allow negative world forces to persist. Right now, your own contribution to the positive forces of the Universe may seem to be trivial, but yours could be the one that tips the delicately balanced scales in favour of planetary survival. You have no way of knowing, any more than a pine tree knows the value of its individual contribution to the air we breathe.

What you can know is that you have a priceless asset that only you can call into play.

You hold the key to a mental powerhouse of unlimited positive potential. Use it.

And be kind to yourself .... every moment of your life.

The circle-breaker at blossom time

"Lost? Of course I'm lost! I was hijacked at birth."
(Camac II)

It is time to confirm an impression that will have arisen from
time to time while you have been practising the self-hypnosis
exercises. You will have experienced a certain feeling of
familiarity, for the simple reason that you have been
hypnotising yourself since birth. Very few of us grow
naturally nowadays. We are shaped. Shaped, cultivated,
conditioned, programmed. It helps to understand
thoroughly, not just superficially, the extent to which we have
been programmed so that we can see what we can do about it.

'The leopard cannot change its spots' is a statement which
more or less makes sense. The nature of the beast can be
modified to some degree if it is trained or conditioned from
an early age, preferably apart from other leopards. However,
even if it is reared with sheep, it will remain a leopard at
heart. It lacks our monkey-like capacity to imitate. Thanks
to this ability and our power to draw on our memories, we
can be made to conform roughly to any social pattern. We
can be shaped to fit. To the extent that we fail to fit the
mould, our reactions can range from irritation and withdrawal to violence and rebellion.

We can readily accept that a child raised in a gypsy caravan
will grow up with a different set of values than the son of a
wealthy nobleman. A child reared in a Hindu home will
differ in outlook from a child born to a Catholic family. And
the child born to a family today will differ from his brother,
born a year earlier. Differ, that is, in conditioning. Differ in
what they each learn to like and dislike, to accept and reject,
to ignore or desire. Differ in the degree of family love, understanding and support they learn to expect and accept as
normal and adequate.

All marriages are mixed marriages, because we each bring
our early conditioning and the subsequent influences of
schooling, work and possibly war into our married lives. We
bring it unconsciously, if only because, in the radiance of

161

new-found love, there is no thought. There is no 'you' and 'me', there is only lovingness, an outpouring, a selflessness, a rarity. To the extent that the love is a love of need or simple sexual attraction, a compulsion rather than a voluntary giving, the relationship is tainted from the start. When thought enters, the glow fades. It is hard to see what you saw in the other person. You have so little in common. You were differently shaped, not only physically but mentally. All you had in common was loneliness and a confused outlook on life.

There is a difficulty in seeing the extent of our conditioning if we think about it. It is our thinking which is conditioned. The circle of conditioned thinking has been formed and has closed on itself. Our thoughts are busily occupied in chewing on their own tails.

What we need to know, for a start, is precisely how and to what extent we have been conditioned and what effect this conditioning has on our daily activities. How is it influencing how we feel in ourselves and how is it affecting our relationships with others? Similarly, what are the differences in the conditioning to which our lifetime partner was exposed and how do they impact on our relationships? What is the right action to take, right now?

We must avoid making any comparisons or judgments of right or wrong. These can only be made from a conditioned viewpoint, by thinking about them. Awareness of the conditioning is the first step and self-hypnosis techniques can help us to achieve the degree of objectivity necessary to transcend conditioned thought. We can start by observing an example of a common relationship event:

'How could you do such a thing to me? You really let me down. I'm disappointed in you.'

How could I do such a thing, a fair question. I chose a course of action which at the time, thanks to the way I have been programmed to think and act, I thought was the thing to do. I was quite aware that the action was ethically or morally unacceptable, but risk-taking has always been part of my make-up and self-discipline has not. I grew up with disrespect for all forms of authority. I have rarely known anyone in authority who is worthy of any respect. I enjoy showing my contempt in all sorts of ways.

So now I appreciate that what I did was done by the conditioned me, the 'me' that I never sought to understand and the 'me' that can only be a surprise to you. You were disappointed because you imagined me to be something else, something more like you. I didn't disappoint you: you disappointed yourself. Up to now, I have always been the conditioned me, unchanging, seemingly unchangeable. From time to time I have tried to live up to your standards but I have a built-in tendency to lapse, to return to my 'natural' style. I see that you have the same difficulty in living up to my standards, some of which you judge as inferior to yours. You seem to be contradictory in many ways, and I suppose I am too. We each have different values. We are probably mentally present about ten-percent of the time at most. The rest of the time we are lost in our separate, conditioned thoughts, lost to one another, lost to the ongoing flow of life.

By quiet contemplation, not by thinking, can I observe the influence of programming in some of my actions and attitudes?

I recall being surprised at how upset and aggressive I can be when an 'opponent' or even a partner in a simple game of tennis seems guilty of a minor breach of what I consider to be good sportsmanship. I appreciate that my reaction could hardly be justified even if we had been gambling for high stakes. When and how was I conditioned to this is the question posed to the subconscious.

The picture comes very clearly to mind of a sportsman father who habitually barracked me whenever we played golf together. He was keen to see me become an unflappable champion, and presumably saw this as a suitable training technique. I resented the barracking as unsportsmanlike, but I never learned how to stop it. Nearly fifty years later, I still react as I should have reacted with my father. The resentment has been kept alive because I failed to deal with the annoyance ... IN THE MOMENT.

So I can accept, as a possibility, that all my thoughts arise from the past; that my past conditioning is responsible for my present actions and that, whatever negative traits I exhibit, I can look to some event in the past to see the sensitising event. My thoughts about the event are the cause of my problem.

When are we free from our bondage to thoughts? When we are happy, truly elated, thought does not enter. In fact, there is only happiness happening, there is no awareness of 'you' and 'me'. Any intense emotion — anger, fear, love — has the same effect of excluding thought. Thought enters later, after the event. Speeding in an automobile, low-flying in an aeroplane, skiing down a mountainside with your life at risk, for a moment you are free from the customary bondage to thought. You are living in the moment, not lost in thought. So the question is, to be free from the past — and all thought comes from the past — must we put our lives at risk? And the answer is yes. The fact is, you have to die to your present way of life.

The question is how deeply do you want to live without anxiety, anger, hate, envy, violence? That you never want to quarrel with anyone again is a trivial aim. Will you still seek to dominate some people and accept a subordinate role with others, seeking to be dependent? Will you continue to draw pleasure from your dislike of some people and things? Will you enjoy criticising, gossiping, making hurtful comments? With what violence and vehemence will you continue to defend your opinions? Will you dedicate yourself to observing what triggers your emotions ... before you react? Make no mistake, this is no place for half-hearted efforts. This is not a ten-day plan for changing your present way of life, of giving the false mask a face-lift. The old way has to go so that you can awaken to the new. If you are seeking vibrant good health, peace of mind and real maturity, that old you has got to die.

We are all part of a society which thought has created. It is riddled with the same imperfections we find in ourselves.

It is a reflection of us and we are a reflection of it. Physically, we are part of it. The question is, can we understand our relationship with society to the extent that we can see what acceptance of the dubious benefits of belonging to some form of group culture can lead to? For example, acceptance of nationalistic programming can lead to violence, to the organised butchery of war.

How do we respond as individuals to frustration, to the failure of people or things to come up to our expectations? By seeking compensations? By going on a shopping spree or by taking our frustrations with us on holiday? By feeding our heads or dulling our senses further with alcohol or drugs? Refer to the group of nine compensation patterns if you need to be reminded of the self-defeating actions we will resort to rather than face up to the real reason for our negative states of mind. Group frustration culminates in suicide and violence, in senseless acts of terrorism. One form of violence, prolonged disregard for the human aspirations of others, leads to the inevitable violent response and the peacemakers become targets for both sides.

Each one of us is a travelling museum of outdated ideas, beliefs and images, none of them original in concept, because all our thoughts have been seeded in us — all our thoughts. On meeting a stranger, we immediately seek to 'place' him, to create a familiar image of him to which we can comfortably relate. 'Where are you from? What do you do? Who do we both know?' And on the basis of the image, we make a judgment, a judgment conditioned by the image we have created of ourselves in the past. We decide 'I like him' or 'I dislike him', though neither of us has met a real person. Two image-makers have exchanged images. We can spend a lifetime with someone and never know the real person or allow the other to know us. Why are we afraid to know someone, or have the someone know us? Because we have never grown up, we have never matured. The mental age of the average intelligent adult, we are told, is fourteen. We are still children, still playing childish games. Dangerous childish games. We start to mature when we start to know ourselves.

How do we lose awareness of ourselves and allow weaknesses to persist? The room you are in at the moment is hopefully familiar to you. Look around it. How many of the things that you can now see around you were not part of your conscious awareness? What is the thing you like best in the room? Did you spare it a glance when you entered? When did you last notice it, how many months ago? That is how conscious you are of familiar things. Most of the time, we are lost in our thoughts. Our thoughts, our ideas, beliefs and opinions stand between us and direct, first-hand experience. Can you look at a sunset without comparison, without judging it against a stored thought, a mental image, a memory of an earlier one? Can you see a person without categorising him in a hundred subtle ways, on the basis of your unique conditioned viewpoint? Knowing that the other person is judging in the same lunatic way? Our normal existence is an unconscious state of self-ignorance, self-denial and self-delusion.

So awareness is knowing this and watching yourself consciously until such time as you awaken your subconscious to act as watchdog for you: watching your relationships, your thoughts and actions with the same intensity of alertness you would apply in driving a car on a narrow mountain trail in a snowstorm. No less dedication and alertness than that.

Patience is still the watchword, operating from your developing centre of calm, always aware that the other person can be quite unconscious of his bias and the deep-seated reasons for its existence. Only you can upset you: have this awareness in your mind at all times.

This does not mean that you have to tolerate rudeness or stupidity on the part of anybody. People have no more right to abuse or belittle you than they have to hit you with a brick. Correct them calmly and firmly, right in the moment. Right in the moment.

As children we learn to tease one another. This is a curiously sly form of expressing hate or envy and some people never outgrow the habit. You can respond with silence or better still, ask what the person really means by his remarks.

It may help him to mature.

What should you always be careful to do when somebody makes a remark or acts in some way to offend your feelings? What is the one and only healthy reaction? Turning the other cheek is an effective response if you are well on the way to cosmic consciousness. Otherwise ignore the insult and the person who insulted you. Take no personal offence but, very carefully, dig deep and find out why you felt hurt. False pride is something that nobody really needs. In *A Journey to Ixtlan*, Carlos Casteneda reports the sound counsel of the Yaqui mystic, Don Juan Matos, "An impeccable hunter makes his weaknesses his prey".

Whenever appropriate, correct people with kindness and patience, without resentment. Be brief and plain-spoken and correct them right in the moment, not later. Just be understanding and never judge or act with an air of superiority. Be grateful that you are learning to master your negative emotions and know that your example conveys more than any attempt to explain the damage they are doing to themselves. They will awaken some day, just as you did. Besides, if you never fall into the error of judging you will find that you are left with nothing to forgive.

It is never enough to question our motives. We must question what is motivating us. Review the situations and comments which have triggered your negative reactions in the past. What loaded and cocked the gun? What are the habitual patterns of argument, aggression and violence which those who have manipulated you are inclined to use? They will use them again and again because their thoughts are chewing on their own tails. They will overreact and say things which have no relation to the real or imagined hurts and resentments which they have failed to clear from their memories: they live with the long-time dead. If they were without false pride and therefore worthy of respect, they would have forgiven all the errors of the past and seen how their own shortcomings contributed to them. Instead, they have judged you without trial and have appointed themselves to punish and manipulate you with perpetual reminders of their perception of your guilt.

You can ask in what respect you have failed to live up to their expectations, and whether it is their purpose in life to live up to yours.

Exaggeration is another childish ploy which is designed to provoke. 'You never listen to what I say. You never think of anyone except yourself. You always make excuses'. Allowing for emotional overkill, discount 'never' to 'very rarely' and 'always' to 'far too often' and accept the outburst as evidence of a problem which patience, kindness and understanding can resolve.

To the exploiter and the artful dodger, your apparently tolerant style may indicate that you are more vulnerable than most, particularly where a special relationship seems to exist, permitting pressure to be applied in the name of family or friendship. For example: 'I hope you don't mind, but your wife said I could borrow the lawn-mower again.' You do mind, because this is the third time, and this is becoming a standard practice. So you confirm that, on this occasion, you don't mind: after all, it is only a minor imposition. However, you feel that the practice should stop before you have to insist on stopping it. 'That way, we can both retain our respect for one another.' If the other person takes offence, it confirms the lack of consideration for your feelings. Friends do not impose on one another. They must always be chosen with care. 'Better alone than in bad company.'

Many people are apparently not yet destined to awaken from their dreamstate, from the ugly world they create as their reality. Stay calm and patient, watchful of your own conditioning. Seek the cause of any remaining destructive tendencies and reactions and eliminate them one by one. With calmness and patience, you cannot hurt yourself or anyone else. See any trials and tribulations as distractions to be overcome. Without constant challenge there would be no possiblility of developing from our infantile mentality to maturity.

With maturity, we learn to accept sole responsibility for our own lives, for every aspect of our lives. Repeating an earlier observation, we do it all to ourselves. Take the example of someone who imposes on your relationship to borrow money, offering the promise of eventual repayment as the only security. All relationships are part of the unstable human drama of role playing, nothing more. Play the role of amateur money-lender, if that is what you decide to choose, but remember that it was your personal choice when, later, you realise that the petitioner sees 'fleecing sheep' as his role in life. That is how he is. Perhaps he became that kind of person when he discovered that the quotation, 'It is better to give than to receive' was inaccurate. The original teaching, in fact, was 'Better than to give or to receive, is to share': a two-way exchange. You will lose two ways if you find yourself resenting that the image you had made of a trustworthy friend or relative was false. If the lesson only costs you part of your savings, you will only have to pay for it once.

As deeper understanding develops, occasional glimpses will be caught of the real responsibilities that everyone is equipped to share. The primary steps are in accepting personal responsibility for everything that happens to you and in forgiving yourself for failing to see the responsibility earlier. This does not mean condoning the ignorance and stupidity in others which contributed to your folly, but it does mean accepting that it was all part of a complex learning experience. 'No snowflake falls in the wrong place' is an apt Zen observation. The reason for our trials and tribulations and how it all fits into the broader picture may never be entirely clear, any more than a blade of grass is likely to be aware that part of its function is to stop the top surface of the mountain from sliding into the valley. Yet it can help initially to see that there is always a right way of handling everyday situations, to appreciate the difference between feeling frustrated or resentful and knowing that two people will have benefited from the way you conducted yourself. And then to forget it, knowing that whether the event happened ten seconds ago or ten thousand years ago, it is past. It has no relevance to now.

A favourite Zen koan on the theme of avoiding strained relationships concerns a visitor to a Buddhist temple, a monk who apparently had learned that nothing in the world is more or less holy than anything else, but had failed to appreciate that there are nevertheless valid reasons for respecting relationships, such as those, for example, that are deemed appropriate between guest and host.

Ignoring a Zen master who was in attendance, the visitor carefully tapped ash from his cigarette on the head of a small statue of Buddha. The Zen master responded spontaneously in such a way that the guest was corrected without offence. What response would you have given to defuse the situation, with patience, kindness and humour?

Stress check. This time, vary the breathing rhythm by inhaling deeply through the nose, expanding the stomach, then the lungs. Hold the breath for the mental count of four, open the mouth and contract the stomach muscles quickly, at the same time expelling all the air. This is an awakening technique, not a relaxation technique. Practise it occasionally until you can do it five or ten times without discomfort.

An interesting story is told of an occasion on which the Lord Buddha was called upon to address a large gathering of people. Taking a rose from a vase in front of him, he held it up to the audience, smiling, saying nothing. Only one man in the audience showed that he understood. He nodded, then laughed. Understanding the unfolding of a rose, what else remains to be understood? The rose knows no discrimination. Its perfume is for everyone. You also have grown from a seed. Do you deny your potential to blossom?

You have borrowed from this Earth, without charge, all that there is of body and mortal mind. From these, you can neither offer nor contribute anything new. Your contribution to evolution can only blossom from your spirit. From spirit you can call forth a radiance to match the perfection inherent in the essence of the rose.

Any questions?

How often should I listen to a self-hypnosis or subliminal persuasion tape for maximum benefit?

Initially I would suggest that you follow the recommendations given in the introduction to each subject. With some subjects, beneficial results are immediately apparent. The most unlikely people often prove to have retained strong imaginative faculties and consequently they respond quickly. An extensive survey of Konicov tape users indicated that only four-per-cent noticed no apparent benefit after listening to a tape on thirty-one occasions.

It depends very much on your past experience whether it takes a long or a short time to neutralise past behaviour patterns and reinforce new behaviour to the extent that it becomes second nature to you. Best results are achieved by keeping within the same tape category — health subjects, for example — before moving to sport, business, educational and other categories.

You will soon find that it pays to devote more time to relaxation techniques as you become more conscious of the valuable living time you waste on escapist novels and television programmes designed to appeal to the herd mind. Aim to widen your reading interests and devote more time to creative hobbies and pastimes. You will be amazed how many worthwhile things there are to do with your life when you decide to accept full responsibility for it.

Do most people lack the ability to achieve full awareness?

Forget most people. Start with yourself. When you have found yourself exposed to unexpected danger, what happened to your awareness? All your senses switched spontaneously to survival mode, right?

Now you are hearing that your own mind has access to unlimited power which can be intentionally or accidentally directed to help you or hurt you. Opportunity on one hand, danger on the other. Now that you are more aware, what do you choose? To disregard it and allow people and events to control your mind, or learn how to condition and control it yourself?

Why are many people afraid of hypnotism?

Firstly, because there is as much fictional nonsense written about hypnotism as there is about love and romance. Then there are critics who have no first-hand experience of it or who, like Freud, failed to learn how to use it. Others, to maintain their positions of power or to support outmoded beliefs, find it pays to promote superstition and fear.

Many experienced health-care specialists use hypnotic techniques effectively, if only to encourage relaxation as an essential part of the healing process. More would do so if they could find more time to devote to individual patients.

As millions of people throughout the world are learning how to use hypnosis, due mainly to the advent of audio cassettes, we can expect to see a refreshing improvement in general understanding over the next few years.

Surely we must first learn to work together to change the corrupt social system before any real progress is possible?

Any change effected by conscious effort carries the seeds of chaos and negativity from the existing system to the next one. This is why all revolutions fail.

First learn how to direct yourself and use all your powers. Start with fifteen minutes of creative relaxation a day, every day, without fail. Fifteen minutes learning how to relax creatively, focusing mental energy in the form of light on various parts of your body, particularly in any areas where you sense discomfort. As your mind moves to open awareness you provide a channel for lifeforce. Direct it wisely and the power made available to you will increase in line with your growing self confidence. This is the greatest contribution you can make to changing the system. As you are, you are part of it. Change one part, you change the whole.

I have a persistent cyst in my mouth which I am told may be malignant. It has to be removed by surgery. What should I do?

Do whatever you decide is best. My personal understanding is that the only malignancy in life is negative thought. I would relax and ponder what minor hurts and annoyances are nagging at me, who or what I am allowing to get under my skin, irritating me to the point of finding that I am constantly nursing the irritation mentally and rehearsing imaginary conversations with the 'culprit'.

Then I would remind myself that everyone and everything is new, as of every new moment of now. Every moment, new, reborn. There is a lesson here for me to see. Forgiveness is required.

I would then decide to cease nursing hurts from the dead past and direct light to soothe and heal and correct the inbalance in the cells over the next two or three days, knowing that whenever I choose to focus positive thought on any part of me, healing energy automatically flows there.

Within three days I would expect to have further evidence of the wisdom of understanding my own inborn curative powers, for my personal benefit and, with increased understanding, for the benefit of those who may seek my help.

Do I have to believe this for it to work?

With a questing mind, you can come to understand. Believe nothing. Belief marks the end of enquiry. Understanding is part of the daily living experience, a product of continuous enquiry.

Beliefs can be explained in words. Understanding is something that dawns on you. You can be guided to understanding by devices like Zen and yoga and hypnosis. When you find that a device works for you, accept, be grateful and move on to still better things, to still deeper understanding, to a higher and higher state of mind. Every moment is a new opportunity. What you need is a genuine desire to change your attitudes and habits.

Apart from belief, does it help to become convinced?

We can convince ourselves of anything and this is part of our problem. Thanks to childhood experiences, we often find it easier to convince ourselves negatively. For example, we can fall into the habit of despising or hating other people. The habitual worrier is a classic example of the power of negative thought. The power of positive thought is even stronger.

So you don't have to be convinced. Any thought that persists in your mind, whether you consider it true or otherwise, eventually percolates through to the subconscious levels and becomes a part of your conditioning. It triggers physical, mental and emotional responses in you and, as like attracts like, it attracts more of the same.

If the effect of the thought is to create tension in you, you bring this tension to every situation you encounter. The problems around you become as much an outgrowth from you as your arms and legs.

Dominant or persistent thoughts necessarily tend towards realisation. Convince yourself of this and see how it works for you.

You say that forgiveness is essential to mental well-being and good health, surely only God has the power to forgive?

Let me expand on a theme which you will recognise. Ignorance of your unlimited personal power for good or ill is forgiven to the same extent that you forgive others. Your trespasses are forgiven to the same degree, no more, no less. In practical terms, to the precise extent that you nurse old hurts and grievances, they hurt you, the whole you, the physical, mental and emotional you.

When you choose to make the dead past a part of you, part of you is dead. Learn how to forgive. It requires the deepest understanding to see the best in yourself and the greatest patience to allow it to develop.

'According to your beliefs it is done unto you'. Go one better, learn to understand. And don't let others think for you or decide what level of understanding you can reach. Your life is your personal responsibility. Accept no limitations.

How do we know if what you say is true?

What have beliefs done for you recently? Do you know yourself enough to believe in yourself? Put your judgmental mind to one side for a moment. Forget all about true or false and decide to test the utility of what is being said, see if it works for you.

What practical value is self hypnosis to a business executive?

Why not resolve to find out for yourself? Knowing about a particular technique is of scant value unless you can apply it to creative purpose. As an executive, you are responsible for making dozens of decisions every day. To what extent are your decisions influenced positively or negatively by subconscious motivations and past conditioning? It could be worthwhile finding out.

Unless you take personal responsibility for conditioning your own mind, other people and events will do it for you. You are fooling yourself if you think you are in charge.

I have chosen the eight things I presently want to achieve in life. How do I ensure that my subconscious will respond?

Specify your aims in eight clear sentences. Then select key words from each and remember them. When you use the affirmation technique, form a mental picture of each requirement as you bring the key words to mind.

To illustrate a reinforcing technique, let me choose three simple aims: a happy family life, a beautiful home by the sea and a cabin cruiser. The idea is to use the advertising man's storyboard technique. Roughly sketch each requirement in three 'boxes' on a sheet of paper or, better still, select appropriate photographs and illustrations from magazines and prepare a one-page collage. Place the storyboard or collage where you can refer to it often until you can visualise each item clearly when you make your affirmations. Your subconscious will get the message.

Is this not encouraging us to be egotistical, even greedy?

Where did that impression originate? Thoughts like 'I suppose I was never meant to be successful' come from the same place.

The miracle of life was not easily attained. It required considerable energy and persistence on your part. Persist now and learn the rules of the lifegame so that you will not be a hazard to yourself and the other players.

Relax and eliminate all negative illusions and limiting thoughts about life. And reserve all judgment, at least until you become an inspiration to yourself and others. You can attain to this and more. Only one person can stop you.

I seem to be catching 'flu. How do I convince myself I'm not?

How would you propose to do that? By arguing vehemently with yourself? Mentally or out loud?

Seriously, if you are actually interested in taking charge of yourself and are not just looking for something else to talk about, you have some understanding to do.

Through relying on what other people think and say, you have absorbed a host of negative, self-limiting beliefs and superstitions. They have become a part of you. They must be dropped. You will get indications from me, not answers. Otherwise you will continue to accept second-hand experiences and fail to awaken your own natural intuitive powers.

So I suggest that you should learn how to stress check and relax, calling on the purple or violet flame to transmute all negative influences and bringing in the mental sunlight to soothe and balance the cells in the area in which discomfort is felt. Because no negative influence can prevail against love, which is the deepest form of human understanding. Wherever you focus it, you bring balance and healing. And the more you do this for yourself and others, the more the lifeforce channel opens and the greater the healing power becomes.

The great healers of the world were born as you were born. Not all of them were selected for special training. Many of them started by asking the kind of questions you have asked today.

What are the principal causes of failure?

Lack of consciousness and too much mental effort. We become lost in our questions.

What can I do about an urge to overeat?

Stress check frequently and relax. Before all meals and whenever you feel empty or experience any sense of lack or loneliness, recognise the feeling as a signal to stress check, relax and drink one or two glasses of warm or cold water. Water is lifeforce in liquid form.

Using the weight control tape, you will find that your weight adjusts to a healthy level without any effort or pressure on your part.

Can the cause of health or emotional problems always be discovered with hypnosis?

Yes, but it is not always essential to know the precise cause. For example, there is no need to work through a particularly unpleasant experience. To see an event with understanding and forgiveness is all that is required. Become aware of the extent to which you have been negatively conditioned since childhood. Worry, anxiety, envy and similar negative emotions can upset the natural rhythm of your heart, lungs and other organs. Watch your thoughts ... transmute the negativity and then do yourself a favour ... get yourself out of your way and see your world unfold. Change your thoughts, you change your destiny.

About the author

Duncan McColl is a Scot who has spent a great deal of his life abroad, mainly in the United States, Canada, Australia, Mexico and Spain.

He served as a pilot/navigator in the RAF in World War II, later qualifying as a chartered accountant and working as a financial and marketing executive in leading British and American companies.

He is a behavioural science instructor, a hypnotist and a life-long student of Zen and comparative religions.

He presently lives with his wife in Shropshire. His son, Peter, lives in Jacksonville, Florida.

PILGRIM conscious self-hypnosis and subliminal response recordings incorporate the latest advances in effective psychotherapy, analytical neuro-linguistic and behavioural science techniques.

Originated by Duncan McColl, MIAPT, FCA, internationally experienced and analytical hypnotherapist, behavioural and management science consultant and author, the ninety-minute audio cassette tapes are acclaimed by health-care professionals and clients worldwide.

The self-improvement and accelerated learning tapes at £12 each are meticulously scripted to promote health understanding, relaxation and stress relief and include past-life experience, fertility, love awareness, creative dreampower and success in study, sport, business and two hundred other subjects.

Tapes are mailed within four days of order and Pilgrim guarantee unconditionally that you will be delighted with the beneficial results.

Brochure and tape selection advice from
PILGRIM TAPES
PO BOX 107,
SHREWSBURY SY1 1ZZ
Telephone: (01743) 821270

Index

Index

Index

Crown House Publishing Limited

Crown Buildings,
Bancyfelin,
Carmarthen, Wales, UK, SA33 5ND.
Telephone: +44 (0) 1267 211880
Facsimile: +44 (0) 1267 211882
e-mail: crownhouse@anglo-american.co.uk
Website: www.anglo-american.co.uk

We trust you enjoyed this title from our range of bestselling books for professional and general readership. All our authors are professionals of many years' experience, and all are highly respected in their own field. We choose our books with care for their content and character, and for the value of their contribution of both new and updated material to their particular field. Here is a list of all our other publications.

Change Management Excellence: Putting NLP To Work In The 21st Century
by Martin Roberts PhD   Hardback   £25.00

Ericksonian Approaches: A Comprehensive Manual
by Rubin Battino & Thomas L South PhD   Hardback   £25.00

Figuring Out People: Design Engineering With Meta-Programs
by Bob G. Bodenhamer & L. Michael Hall   Paperback   £12.99

Gold Counselling™: A Practical Psychology With NLP
by Georges Philips & Lyn Buncher   Paperback   £14.99

Grieve No More, Beloved: The Book Of Delight
by Ormond McGill   Hardback   £9.99

Hypnotherapy Training In The UK: An Investigation Into The Development Of
    Clinical Hypnosis Training Post-1971
by Shaun Brookhouse   Spiralbound   £9.99

Influencing With Integrity: Management Skills For Communication & Negotiation
by Genie Z Laborde   Paperback   £12.50

A Multiple Intelligences Road To An ELT Classroom
by Michael Berman   Paperback   £19.99

Multiple Intelligences Poster Set
by Jenny Maddern   Nine posters   £19.99

The New Encyclopedia Of Stage Hypnotism
by Ormond McGill   Hardback   £29.99

NOW It's Your Turn For Success! Training And Motivational Techniques For Direct Sales And
    Multi-Level Marketing
by Richard Houghton and Janet Kelly   Paperback   £9.99

Peace Of Mind Is A Piece Of Cake
by Michael Mallows & Joseph Sinclair   Paperback   £8.99

The POWER Process: An NLP Approach To Writing
by Sid Jacobson & Dixie Elise Hickman   Paperback   £12.99

Precision Therapy: A Professional Manual Of Fast And Effective Hypnoanalysis Techniques
by Duncan McColl PhD   Paperback   £15.00

Scripts & Strategies In Hypnotherapy
by Roger P. Allen   Hardback   £19.99

The Secrets Of Magic: *Communicational Excellence For The 21st Century*
by L. Michael Hall   Paperback   £14.99

Seeing The Unseen: *A Past Life Revealed Through Hypnotic Regression*
by Ormond McGill   Paperback   £12.99

Slimming With Pete: *Taking The Weight Off Body AND Mind*
by Pete Cohen & Judith Verity   Paperback   £9.99

Smoke-Free And No Buts!
by Geoff Ibbotson & Ann Williamson   Paperback   £7.99

Solution States: *A Course In Solving Problems In Business With The Power Of NLP*
by Sid Jacobson   Paperback   £12.99

The Sourcebook Of Magic: *A Comprehensive Guide To NLP Techniques*
by L. Michael Hall   Paperback   £14.99

The Spirit Of NLP: *The Process, Meaning And Criteria For Mastering NLP*
by L. Michael Hall   Paperback   £12.99

Sporting Excellence: *Optimising Sports Performance Using NLP*
by Ted Garratt   Paperback   £9.99

Time-Lining: *Patterns For Adventuring In "Time"*
by Bob G. Bodenhamer & L. Michael Hall   Paperback   £14.99

The User's Manual For The Brain: *The Complete Manual For Neuro-Linguistic Programming
    Practitioner Certification*
by Bob G. Bodenhamer & L. Michael Hall   A4 binder   £35.00

Vibrations For Health And Happiness: *Everyone's Easy Guide To Stress-free Living*
by Tom Bolton   Paperback   £9.99

see overleaf for order form

Order form
********Special offer: 4 for the price of 3!!!********

Buy 3 books & we'll give you a 4th title - FREE!
(free title will be book of lowest value)

Qty	Title		Qty	Title
—	Change Management Excellence		—	The POWER Process
—	Ericksonian Approaches		—	Precision Therapy
—	Figuring Out People		—	Scripts & Strategies In Hypnotherapy
—	Gold Counselling™		—	The Secrets Of Magic
—	Grieve No More, Beloved		—	Seeing The Unseen
—	Hypnotherapy Training In The UK		—	Slimming With Pete
—	Influencing With Integrity		—	Smoke-Free And No Buts!
—	The Magic Of Mind Power		—	Solution States
—	A Multiple Intelligences Road To An ELT		—	The Sourcebook Of Magic
	Classroom		—	The Spirit Of NLP
—	Multiple Intelligences Poster Set		—	Sporting Excellence
—	New Encyclopedia Of Stage Hypnotism		—	Time-Lining
—	Now It's YOUR Turn For Success!		—	The User's Manual For The Brain
—	Peace Of Mind Is A Piece Of Cake		—	Vibrations For Health And Happiness

Postage and packing

UK:	£2.50 per book
	£4.50 for two or more books
Europe:	£3.50 per book
Rest of the world	£4.50 per book

My details:

Name: Mr/Mrs/Ms/Other (please specify) ....

Address: ....

....

....

Postcode: ....Daytime tel: ....

I wish to pay by:

❏ Amex   ❏ Visa   ❏ Mastercard   ❏ Switch – Issue no./Start date: ....

Card number:...Expiry date:...................................

Name on card:...Signature:...

❏ cheque/postal order payable to **AA Books**

Please send me the following catalogues:

❏ Accelerated Learning (Teaching Resources)	❏ Psychotherapy/Counselling
❏ Accelerated Learning (Personal Growth)	❏ Employment Development
❏ Neuro-Linguistic Programming	❏ Business
❏ NLP Video Library – hire (UK only)	❏ Freud
❏ NLP Video Library – sales	❏ Jung
❏ Ericksonian Hypnotherapy	❏ Transactional Analysis
❏ Classical Hypnosis	❏ Parenting
❏ Gestalt Therapy	❏ Special Needs

Please fax/send to:
The Anglo American Book Company,
FREEPOST SS1340
Crown Buildings, Bancyfelin,
Carmarthen, West Wales,
United Kingdom, SA33 4ZZ,
Tel: +44 (0) 1267 211880/211886 Fax: +44 (0) 1267 211882
or e-mail your order to:
crownhouse@anglo-american.co.uk